Resistant Hope

Resistant Hope
Fighting Back against Suffering

Elaine G. Siemsen

WIPF & STOCK · Eugene, Oregon

RESISTANT HOPE
Fighting Back against Suffering

Copyright © 2008 Elaine G. Siemsen. All rights reserved. Except for brief quotations in critical publications or reviews, no part of this book may be reproduced in any manner without prior written permission from the publisher. Write: Permissions, Wipf and Stock Publishers, 199 W. 8th Ave., Suite 3, Eugene, OR 97401.

ISBN 13: 978-1-55635-287-4
Manufactured in the U.S.A.

Scripture quotations from HarperCollins Study Bible, Society of Biblical Literature, New York: 2006. Harold W. Attridge, editor.

This work is dedicated to Dennis, Amelia, and Erin, who support me in my struggle to write, humor me in my crabby moods, and celebrate with me in times of success. In addition to my family, I offer thanks to the many students and friends who have contributed to this work in ways that are too numerous to name. Finally, this work is indebted to the theological work of Joseph Sittler and those who have followed in his path.

Contents

Introduction ix

Chapter 1: Everyone Suffers 1

Chapter 2: What Does God Have to Do with This? 15

Chapter 3: Scripture and Tradition: What Does the Bible Say? 28

Chapter 4: Becoming: God's Goal for the Creation 41

Chapter 5: Resistance through Hope 59

Chapter 6: The Beginning 71

Glossary of Terms 75

Bibliography and Recommended Reading List 81

Introduction

THERE ARE MANY BOOKS available on the market designed to help us through times of suffering. They all offer answers and proposals as to why we suffer, what purpose is to be found in this experience, and how can we go forward after our life has been shattered. It is reasonable to ask what I think I am going to add to all of these ideas.

I have spent several years teaching and writing about suffering and a concept in Christian theology called theodicy. Interest in the question of suffering began as I learned the answers proposed by Christian theology. As I tried to apply those answers to the painful experiences in my life, I was left feeling hollow and sad.

Through teaching, I had the opportunity to share my frustrations and questions with students of all ages and backgrounds. In return, these students contributed to my ideas and helped to shape this text. With anger and with tears, they shared their personal stories of pain and suffering. Together we struggled to find a method that would allow us to recover God's promised hope.

Seeking hope is a common thread in all the stories. For our generation and all generations, the victims of suffering demand that the teachers of the church show us a way to understand suffering. The most common teachings approach the subject of suffering from the perspective of defending God. Along this path the great and not-so-great thinkers of the Christian community desire two things. First, they wish to avoid the human practice of blaming God for their suffering. Second, they reject or at least modify the temptation to hold God responsible for the pain they have experienced. There have been a couple of notable exceptions. C. S. Lewis wanted the reader to believe that God sent and used pain as a means of correcting the wandering, wayward believer. At least this seems to be the position of Lewis in his first book on suffering, *The Problem of Pain*.

Introduction

This book is not about defending God. I believe that God does not need my defense. This book is about how God, alone and through us, comes when we suffer to rescue us from the abyss of despair. Through my personal experience and time spent with others at moments of suffering, I have heard many either blame God or accept with painful resignation that God had sent this devastating pain. When individuals were controlled by these positions, I watched them slide into the dark abyss of hopelessness. One Sunday morning, this abyss was obvious to all before worship services began.

A STORY

When the young wife died of uterine cancer, her husband and two children sought refuge in the family of their church congregation. Medicine had no answers as to why it was his wife, their mother, who died. As they began to emerge into the light of the love of friends, one Sunday they returned to church. They were met at the door of the church by a member who held that suffering was sent by God but could be prevented through ardent and faithful prayer. His opening greeting to the grieving husband was, "I don't know why God sent this sadness to you. Maybe if you had prayed harder, God would have saved her life." The young father began to weep silently. Taking his children by the hands, he turned back to his car. The hopelessness of suffering had followed him to this place of worship. He was now confirmed in his belief that he had failed his wife, children, and even God.

This is not a story about the God of scripture or of the Christ of salvation. However, stories and experiences such as this are rooted in the teaching and preaching of the Christian tradition. This experience over twenty years ago now continues to bring me great sadness. At the time, I did not know what to say. I just knew that the church member was wrong. Now many years later, it is my hope that at the conclusion of these writings you will find a pathway to revealing hope in the midst of the pain of daily life and at the moments of greatest grief and sorrow. This hope is not a false assurance of easy Christianity. It is the hope of God through Christ that speaks to us through the scriptures and the teachings of the church.

How will I accomplish that? Chapter One leads us into understanding the present answers and their devastating effects upon those who suffer. This task begins by defining suffering. Actually, that is a task that is

Introduction

beyond words. So it begins with describing the effects of suffering. There are many thoughtful people who have provided descriptions of the effects of suffering upon humanity. These ideas are gathered together to set the stage for finding hope. Chapter One examines the relationship of suffering to evil. This is a serious dilemma for many Christians. It is hard to know which comes first: evil or suffering. It probably does not matter. We need to understand the effect as the two destroy our lives.

As I mentioned above, there have been many attempts to describe the source or cause of suffering. Most attempts are really attempts to defend God. Chapter Two takes a careful look at the four proposals that stand as answers to suffering. These theological ideas have become predictable parts of Christian responses to people who are in pain. Each answer seems logical on the surface. However, with in-depth consideration, we will see how they lead us further away from God and consequently further away from hope.

There is a long history of Christian thinking that comes along with the application of these four responses. Chapter Three takes us back to the source that informs all the teachings of Christianity: the Holy Bible. What does God have to say about the nature of humanity, the course of suffering, and suffering's devastating effects upon humanity and the entire creation?

Chapter Three begins with a brief outline of how Christianity got itself into this situation. The examination of scripture begins with Genesis, moves into the writings of Paul, and finally ends in the interpretation by church teachers. The chapter examines the continuing power of Christian teaching. The conclusion of Chapter Three demonstrates that when Christians tell only part of the faith story or speak of God from only one tradition, people of faith are oppressed by their own trust in God as both loving and all powerful.

Chapter Four invites us to approach the experiences of human suffering from a different perspective. Having established a definition of the effects of suffering and come to understand the traditional and familiar answers, it is time to build a new response to the experience of suffering. Of course, this is not really a new response. It is a very old response that begins by looking carefully at God's goal for creation. This is the point to introduce many readers to a teacher of the Church whose writings are not known to most people who are not a part of the Eastern Orthodox community. Irenaeus of Lyon wrote in the third century. His writings

Introduction

contain wonderful explanations of God's goal for all creation. Utilizing three steps, Irenaeus shows that as we embrace the life and work of Jesus the Christ, we get a glimpse into God's plan and goal for creation.

The first step examines God's plan or creation. This is a plan of love and compassion. The second step in finding hope is naming the reality that human action has interfered with God's plan. In traditional Christian language, this is naming the sin or brokenness that taints the creation. Again, many great thinkers have described the effects of sin as chaos and disharmony that destroys the ability of creation, human and otherwise, to move toward God. The brokenness of life traps us in a repeating cycle of tragedy and pain. We are tempted to rejoice that our suffering is not a great as another, to pretend that suffering does not exist, or to callously dismiss the pain or others as somehow deserved or even invited.

In the third step, attention focuses on the life and death of Jesus Christ. Here God reveals all human answers to suffering are drawn from the human community. In Jesus we learn that accepting human answers as truth traps us into a cycle of guilt that destroys the very human nature within each of us. The gift of Christ is the power to break free of our humanly imposed barriers. The way to hope in the midst of suffering is found by returning to the beginning. God has never ceased to love and bless the creation. God has never ceased to call the children of God good and blessed. Now those are two claims that will need further explanation.

Too often we confuse the consequences of our actions for a condemnation from God of our human existence. In times of suffering, we also lose sight that God created humanity with the purpose to work with God to achieve God's goal and purpose. Here we must look carefully at the work and life of Christ. In Chapter Five we uncover how Christ shows us the path to work with God in the power of God's compassionate love to impact the effects of suffering. Christ shows us how to resist the effects of suffering and evil. It is in this resistance that we find hope for ourselves and bring hope to the creation.

There are three actions for building Resistant Hope to the effects of suffering/evil. In Chapter Five, these are explored. The first action is to look for God. Suffering/evil works to blind the victims to the actions and activity of God. The faith community constantly identifies God's actions in creation to assist the victims. The second action is to reject passivity. As suffering/evil gains control in life, it advances by reducing victims to pas-

Introduction

sive acceptance of its control. Rejecting the resulting passivity begins by naming our actions and the actions of others that lead to suffering/evil.

The third action of Resistant Hope is to fight back against suffering/evil. Chapter Five explores how fighting back is powered by God's compassionate love. Fighting back through Resistant Hope recognizes three steps: affirming God's loving nature, assessing human immaturity, and accepting Christ's initiation of a new path.

This book does not offer a pathway or a plan to eliminate or eradicate all the suffering. This is not even a plan for minimizing the pain that an individual experiences in the course of his or her lifetime. This is a different kind of Christian "how-to" book. This is a book about fighting back. Christians have often chosen to see their faith as either a blanket to cover the pain of life or an answer book that gives explanation to suffering. I believe that God is active through us and desires that we fight back against the evil and suffering in this world. This fighting back is not about gaining something that we think we deserve. We fight back because it is God's will, desire, and plan that all creation live in justice and love united with God. This book is about reclaiming the power of God's compassionate love in the example of Christ to shape who we are and to influence the world around us.

This book invites you to journey with other readers. This journey will not come to a satisfactory conclusion. Suffering will not end because we accept the call to resist suffering/evil. Victims will continue even though Christians name the evil within our own lives. There will be a rise in hope. Individually and communally, hope will increase our ability to be truly human.

One step that will assist in moving humanity forward is for each reader to make the experiences of this book personal. At the conclusion of each section, there are a few questions. These are designed to assist you in bringing the ideas of the section into direct conversation with your personal experience of suffering. The second purpose of these questions is to assist each reader to make a connection with another victim of suffering.

1

Everyone Suffers

It happens all the time: on the elevator, in the store, at the party. People begin to share life events of pain that continue to shape and influence their lives. It was in the bookstore and the woman next to me in the Romance aisle began to share about her child's drug problem. She talked with anger about how it had nearly ruined the family financially as well as emotionally. I was at the baseball game and a man there began with questions about why God allows disease and finished with the story of his mother's illness. The college student came in for conversation about her paper but really wanted to talk about her roommate's verbal abuse that included ridicule, leaving this young woman feeling worthless. The child spoke about the fear that a family crisis was his fault. In each life suffering had damaged a wonderful individual. Each person, as a child of God, needs to reclaim his or her life through pushing back at the devastation left by suffering.

The stories are all as unique as the individuals. If you have picked up this book, you also have a story that is as unique as you are. Each person who reads this text has his or her own story of suffering and its effects.

DISPELLING MYTHS

As a society, we often think there is an age requirement for understanding suffering. We attribute it to the older, more experienced members of the community. Somehow the number of years lived gives validation to the explanation of suffering. Yet generations of people have been overwhelmed by emotion while reading *The Diary of Anne Frank*. On the lighter side, we have been sadly amused by the misfortunes of the Baudelaire children in *A Series of Unfortunate Events* by Lemony Snicket.

News stories from the Sudan to China or the streets of Chicago show us that there is no age requirement for suffering. In our desperate search for answers and meaning, we turn on each other. The senior citizen at the adult Sunday school class dismissed the pain of the younger participants, saying, "You have not lived long enough to know what real suffering is." The anguished fifth grader quietly spoke to the teacher and parent, saying, "You don't understand what I am feeling because you are too old!"

This first communal myth is false. Even the youngest among us have experienced the pain and change that comes from suffering. We have all seen or personally experienced an encounter with a young person whose life has been severely limited by disease or congenital conditions. Here we see obvious signs of suffering. We learn about emergency room trips or frequent hospital stays.

There are, however, many children who suffer from the careless words of adults who call them stupid or ridicule a budding talent or youthful attempt at a sport. There are children who hide the effects of suffering behind cheerful smiles and helpful attitudes. I know this position personally. In my family, my father was an alcoholic, and my mother pretended there was no problem. The verbal arguments were legendary in proportion. Though there was no physical abuse, I suffered from the anger and hostility that would control our family when my father drank. My response was to be the "perfect" child. I put on a cheerful face and worked hard to please teachers, friends, and even my parents. Most of my friends and teachers had no idea how painful our household could be at times. For a long time, no one saw that suffering was changing me on a daily basis.

The suffering of an older person can be as easily dismissed. We expect people over twenty-five, or nowadays thirty, to act responsibly and well, be grown-up. When a friend weeps at the frustration of life and job, she is likely to be told to just put up with it. When a guy vents his anger on the soccer field, no one looks much deeper for the cause, accepting the venting, but not really wanting to see the pain. When week after week the woman in Sunday school mentions the frequent headaches and chronic fatigue, we ask if she has seen the physician, because we look for an organic cause. However, we do not, as a rule, ask her about the death of her child. After all, that happened years ago.

As we look at the elderly, too little respect or recognition is given to the sorrow caused by diminishing physical abilities, such as a reduced ability to move or loss of eyesight. Careless comments about diminished capacities are accepted with humor. We fail to look deeper into the signs of depression caused by suffering. The sense of a burdened life is accepted as a sign of aging.

In all cases of suffering, we see the effects but fail to look for the cause. We want to avoid the truth that we humans are frail and that suffering damages us. Our action of avoidance is as harmful as the suffering itself. However, our response is almost understandable. When we carefully look at suffering, that of ourselves and of others, two things happen. First, it reveals a truth about ourselves and others that we prefer to avoid. We see our contribution to the destruction of others. In addition, when we see suffering for what it is, a destruction of humanity, we face our greatest fear: that we are helpless to confront or respond to the destruction.

However, when we take a critical look at the experiences of suffering, we see two common characteristics. In all stories, all experiences, no matter the age of the individual, we see that suffering changes the life of the individual forever. The result of suffering is that it reshapes how we see ourselves and the world. To find a metaphor, suffering distorts the lens through which we view life. Second, suffering brings physical, emotional, and even monetary destruction into each life, family, and community.

WHAT IS SUFFERING?

So what is suffering? Comedians throw away the word "suffering" when the audience fails to laugh. A quick Internet search on the phrase, "I'm suffering here," brings millions of hits, most of which are about personal achievement or desires. Suffering is a word most often used to describe those times when we fail to get what we want. It is associated with the unpleasant consequences of reasonable restrictions enforced by parents, bosses, or others. "I'm suffering here," has become the battle cry of overindulged, self-focused people who really mean, "I'm not getting what I want here." These are selfish uses of the term and distort its true meaning. Like all cultural derivations, there is some truth to these popular expressions. Even in the cry of the most spoiled and whining person, we understand that suffering is associated with deprivation and pain.

But is all pain suffering? No, it is not. There is pain that is the result of a physical stimulus that actually brings knowledge into our lives. This type of pain offers us warnings for everything from minor injuries to possible disaster. It can be experienced as random and unpredictable, but usually a source can be identified. Without this type of pain, we would inevitably cause greater harm to ourselves and to others. C.S. Lewis proposed that we know that this type of pain is not true suffering because of the difference of its intensity.

This might be the pain that comes from touching the flame of a candle or the pain of a skinned knee from a fall off a bicycle. Some pain leads us to our becoming more human. Through this pain, we learn that there are limits to our human abilities. Through this we both restrict and stretch our goals. For example, in the very young or very old, the pain of a fall teaches that there are limits to mobility. Ella shows us her bandaged knees in an appeal to understand her suffering. The two-year-old might learn to resist the temptation to jump from the high steps to the concrete sidewalk at the front of the house. The elderly person learns that the loose rugs on the kitchen floor are a danger. For the athlete, the pain of sore muscles teaches that a different kind of exercise or activity is necessary so that the body will not experience this type of pain again. Pain in these settings, like the athlete, both shows us the limits and expands the potential of the physical activity.

This type of pain contributes to our becoming more fully human. It is one part of our learning both the limits and the possibilities within our lives. Pain of this sort is never absent from our lives. There are always learning experiences that can seem painful and yet that assist us in being creative creatures. Creativity and risk come into our lives at a cost. Whether it is reaching out to make a new friend on the playground at school, the first day on a new job, becoming an Olympic champion, or being the local soccer hero, there is a cost.

The pain from risks is a part of the creative plan of God. It is the pain of becoming and growing. God does not send this pain to teach us a lesson or to correct our behaviors. God does, however, know that this pain is the result of our actions. The divine creator knows the limits on the frail vessel that we call our body. The body does not always bend to our demands. Sometimes it breaks. God also knows that learning can be a painful process.

The pain of becoming and growing also occurs when the human desire to be in control leads us into places where we will be hurt. This pain reminds us that not all our human desires are healthy, life affirming, and even good. In the end, God knows that great things—art, ideas, accomplishments—do not come without a price. As popular wisdom reminds us, "There are no free rides." God knows that for us to become the humanity that God created us to be, there will be pain. Ultimately the pain of becoming and growing is a part of the story of our life.

At the store, school, work, or even church we exchange our life stories with each other. It is not to gloat exactly. Rather, this kind of pain is so common to us that we speak of it openly. As we swap these stories with each other, we attempt to find meaning in our lives. We learn the lessons of life through sharing these stories. As Nancy sported a new cast in church on Sunday, she could assure all, young and old, that one should not stand on a chair to wash the windows.

There is, however, in the lives of all people another kind of pain of greater intensity. This pain is described as anguish or adversity because of its ability to bring total disruption to the order and structure of life. In its early stages, as this pain devours its victim, there is the desire to find meaning in this moment of suffering. In the first few days or weeks, as this pain accompanies them, people try to push past the experience to find answers. This is the pain that I often hear from the victim of abuse, the cancer survivor, and the victim of violence.

As we observe others on the commuter train, at work, at school, or at the doctor's office, we can see the difference. The stories of this pain begin or end with the cry, "Why did this happen?" The lives of these sufferers have been disturbed or even destroyed by the random and seemingly unfair distribution of pain that really is suffering. Their stories stop our complaints cold. The headlines from the Internet or the local newspaper scream at us that suffering of others has exceeded our imaginations. We cannot compare the pain of becoming and growing with the pain of a school shooting. Our health issues cannot be compared to a deranged mother killing her children. Even a failed work of our creative imaginations cannot be compared to the cost of life in war and genocide.

This pain of greater intensity or suffering breaks the spirit of the victim, as he or she fails to find an answer to the question of meaning. This is the pain of suffering that is more than a physical warning of future error. It gives rise to the feelings that there is no hope in the world. It blocks all attempts to find meaning. When this pain enters, it creates disorder where there was once a pattern and structure of meaning. Suddenly, the pieces of life do not fit together.

Ultimately, anguish-suffering blinds the victims so that all that they can see is the repetitious patterns of abuse, pain, and suffering. The focus of the sufferer narrows inward upon the experience and effects of the pain. All actions and all attempts to break free increase the pain. The imagination shuts down, accepting suffering as both inevitable and deserved. When anguish-suffering takes hold of a life, all hope dies and the lies of the pain rule.

In these situations of anguish-suffering within our lives and in the world, common questions are heard. "Why does this happen to me, to others, in the world?" "What is wrong with people in the world?" "Can nothing be done?" And finally some will cry out, "Where is God?"

Religious leaders and people of faith heard these questions on 9/11. As candles were lit in memory, college students demanded answers for the shootings at Virginia Tech. Hometown friends spoke these questions quietly when an innocent child was shot while playing on the front porch of her family home.

The temptation is to stop at this point and try to answer these compelling questions. To do so, to try to find answers, is getting ahead of our story. Before exploring the source of anguish-suffering, we need to try and create a workable definition of suffering. Merriam-Webster Online dictionary offers words that are supposed to define suffering. It reads that suffering means to submit, be forced to endure, to put up with something that is inevitable or unavoidable.

In light of human experience, this definition seems too simple, too casual, too superficial. It is the kind of definition that applies to missing a toy or television show or even missing a meal. We know that suffering is much more than this. The definition demonstrates to us the difficulty in defining the word. The true meaning of suffering cannot be defined. It can only be experienced through our description of its effects.

Christian Beker writes:

> Suffering indeed stuns and numbs us. The blows and arrows of outrageous fate either strike us with unexpected ferocity or wear us down with unrelenting persistence. Suffering attacks the core of our being.[1]

Anguish-suffering changes everything in our world. We are no longer the same. Our very essence has been lost. All sources agree that suffering

---

1. Beker, *Suffering and Hope*, 80.

indicates that something has been taken away from the individual, family, or community. There are some who would say that we suffer because pain and evil are the dominant or controlling powers within human life. I disagree. We suffer because we have physical, psychological, and certainly religious knowledge that there is something better.

As a brief introduction to a topic that will appear later in the text, Christianity affirms that human creation is the both the creation of God and blessed by God. We recognize suffering because we were created to know that God has chosen and blessed us. In other words, because we were created to know God's love, we suffer when we are separated or isolated and cannot find that love.

With this assumption, suffering is then the deprivation of this blessing. Through its power, suffering takes away our psychological, emotional, and even physical sense of God's power and blessing. Suffering is an attack to the heart, the center of human identity. Ultimately suffering destroys our ability to accept God's love, to trust in the love of others, and to even love ourselves. The ultimate goal of suffering is to block all hope. When love cannot get though to the sufferer, the result is the spiraling darkness of life without hope.

Theologian Dorothee Soelle wrote that suffering attacks us psychologically as well as physically. Psychological sources of suffering range from oppressive work situations to the emotional abuse of family and personal relationships. Psychological suffering is characterized by a reduction of hope in relationship to personal success and advancement.[2] Many experience this type of suffering every day. The voice of the supervisor brings on a headache even when he or she is speaking to someone else. The thought of an annual review or job evaluation brings on physical illness. The constant fear of conflict at the dinner table brings on hives on the way to school.

This form of suffering is often well hidden. Society teaches us that we are not to speak about the difficulties of job or family situations. When these sufferings are revealed, the individual is often labeled as uncooperative or the betrayer of the family. Suffering and our social response to it push the individual into isolation. This isolation leads to emotional death. As the sufferer turns inward, his or her ability to communicate with others is completely destroyed.

---

2. Sölle, *Suffering*, 65.

The victim of psychological attack, now isolated, is mute. There is no language to explain the pain. There are no words to explain hope that has died.[3] The death of hope contributes to the power of suffering, which now is able to go even further. As hope dies, any positive experience, any good feelings, any creative abilities are hidden from the sight of the sufferer. The sufferer's vision is narrowed. They now see only the painful. They are always on the lookout for the next attack even behind the kind words of a loving God.

The result of this form of suffering is silence. Of course these people are not physically silent. They attempt to continue on through their day. As a day, week, month, and year moves forward, they pretend to travel with the world as they hide behind a screen. When asked, they go to great lengths to assure the world that they are satisfied with life. This self-protective measure is adopted because suffering has convinced them that there is no chance of change.

So how does it work? According to Jewish writer Emmanuel Levinas, suffering is a noun, and it describes a consciousness. It has content like any other lived experience. Suffering has color, sound, and contact like any other sensation. Unlike the experience of eating ice cream or receiving a hug, suffering is unwanted because it pushes into our innermost self. Suffering has the ability to graft onto all the other experiences in our consciousness. It is like a parasite that feeds and lives off of every other feeling, emotion, desire, and idea that makes us who we are.

Suffering is a rape of the senses.[4] The harshness of this label only begins to give voice to the destructive power of suffering. As rape, it carries three characteristics. First, suffering is un-welcomed. Victims do not invite suffering into their lives. Suffering is not something that they have added to their identities so that they can better understand themselves or the world. Suffering does not bring value into the individual life action of seeking meaning.

Second, suffering forces a kind of submission upon its victim. The victim is controlled by the passivity of suffering. This is not, Levinas writes, passivity that is the opposite of action. Suffering reduces the victim beyond inaction. The victim has no choice for freedom or action. Suffering has taken everything from him. All he is left with is the total

---

3. Sölle, *Suffering*, 69.
4. Levinas, entre nous, 92.

elimination or obstruction of any kind of personal freedom or meaning. Suffering has reduced the victim to a place of nonbeing.

Finally, suffering is useless. Suffering brings no value into the life of the victim. There is no meaning that can be pulled or culled out of the experience of suffering. Suffering is so powerful that the victim is reduced to the psychological, religious, and even physical experience of total abandonment and hopelessness. Suffering is useless because in the consciousness of the victim of such violence, there is no longer an opening for the mercy of God through others to make an entrance. In other words, for the sufferer there is no way out.

Levinas convinces us that this suffering is evil. It results in creating a place or consciousness of total loss within individuals or even entire communities. This suffering/evil leaves humanity isolated, lost to any sense of personal value, and mute with despair. Suffering/evil reinforces the physical and emotional belief that God has abandoned the sufferer. Evil is death, infecting life.

Wendy Farley calls suffering/evil "radical suffering." This description of evil describes the power within suffering/evil to dominate the victim. "Evil gratuitously hurts and disrupts human existence."[5] The power that evil exerts causes damage or even destroys the chance for a hope-filled life. It is not evil when physical pain or illness leads to death. All humanity is mortal. It is evil when the "spark of life and dignity can be snuffed out in them [human beings] before they die."[6]

Amnesty International tells us of radical evil as they describe the horror lived out daily by child soldiers in Africa. They report that as of 2007, worldwide, more than half a million children under eighteen have been recruited into government armed forces, paramilitaries, civil militias, and a variety of non-state armed groups in more than eighty-five countries. When Albert was fifteen, armed opposition in the Democratic Republic of Congo (DRC) recruited him. He reports:

> [T]hey would give us "chanvre" [cannabis] and force us to kill people to toughen us up. Sometimes they brought us women and girls to rape . . . They would beat us if we refused.[7]

---

5. Farley, *Tragic Vision*, 40.
6. Farley, 41.
7. http://www.amnesty.org/childsoldiers.

WHERE DOES SUFFERING/EVIL COME FROM?

It is not evil that humans will become ill. It is not evil that humans will treat each other with casual disregard or disrespect. It is evil that we have the power and ability to cripple the human spirit of another. So where does this ability come from? The responses to this question are many and varied. A quick search at the online booksellers will produce many volumes that tell us about the cause or source of suffering. Many of these approach the subject through the teachings of Buddhism. As one author writes:

> Suffering, the Buddha taught, is caused when the freedom that is inherent to our nonlocal pristine awareness is obscured by the limitations of our ego and our physical body. We forget that we are pure awareness, residing only for a time as a physical body.[8]

Christianity has a long history of trying to answer this question with practical experience and recognizable human actions. In a simple form, suffering exists because human freedom exists. Choices that individuals and communities make always carry the possibility of being the source of suffering/evil directed at others outside of themselves.

In an attempt to describe how freedom works to result in suffering/evil, Dorothee Soelle writes that there are identifiers that show the suffering/evil is the result of particular uses of human freedom. She calls these markers of evil. By this she means that there are human behaviors that are accepted by most of society and actually serve to hide the evil within each of us. There are at least three ways to describe these makers. The first marker is self-deception. The second is the callous disregard of the pain of others. The third marker is our human bondage to evil.

Self-deception is one way that we disguise evil. Through it we are trying to protect ourselves. Using self-deception, we choose to believe that our life is undisturbed by the suffering that is happening around us. We feel sorry for those who suffer but fail to see how a child soldier in Africa or a monk dying in Myanmar has any impact on the quality of our lives. Self-deception is a sign that we are willing to be seduced by evil. We accept and even approve of the lies that the world presents to us. The evil of self-deception is demonstrated by the words that we choose to describe

---

8. Tarq, Hurtak, *The End of Suffering*, 6.

the evil in the world. We choose words that disguise the horror: murder is sterilized into simple death, and rape is sanitized into sexual abuse.

Even when we are using self-deception to sanitize evil, we can further delude ourselves into accepting our actions as safe ways to confront evil. We believe that if we avoid naming the atrocity, we can somehow reduce its effect upon the victims. We believe the college student who was attacked will get over her pain much faster if we avoid the term "rape." The sad truth about self-deception is that we participate in inflicting more suffering/evil upon the victims when we convince ourselves that we are sparing them through our deceptions.

How can this be? Most people who are kind and good do not want to hurt the victims any more than they are already suffering. However, suffering/evil flourishes when we hide it in the darkness of our own creating. Scripture repeatedly uses darkness as the metaphor for all that destroys humanity and creation. We know in our own bodies that a hidden sore can fester and poison the rest of a limb. To bring healing, suffering must be brought into the light of compassion and love. Self-deception is like a greenhouse for the propagation of suffering/evil.

The second marker of suffering/evil is callousness. While we can praise what seems to be an intrinsic ability within humanity to recognize and respond to the suffering of others, there is also the ability to ignore that same suffering. Through the marker of callousness, spontaneous concern is replaced with apathy toward the suffering of others. Through callousness, energies that empower instincts to protect or defend are diverted into active avoidance.

We exhibit our callousness when we stand by and watch as power is misused against the innocent, doing or saying nothing. It is callousness that encourages us to criticize the verbally abusive parent but to avoid stepping into the fight to save a child from a beating. In fact, the enormous misuse of power resulting in terrible cruelties becomes possible when we turn away with callous dismissal of the cause of others. History documents the callousness of entire nations that allowed for the suffering/evil of oppression to flourish during times of war.

The danger of the marker of callousness is that it can be hidden behind the words, "I can't get involved." Or, "It is none of my business." Or even worse, "There is nothing that I can do." Suffering/evil can capitalize upon our fears, convincing us that our words are true and not just an excuse. This marker of suffering/evil is so successful that it does not take long until we and the victim believe the lie that there is nothing that can be done to stop the suffering.

Like all the markers of suffering/evil, callousness does not completely eradicate the human desire for justice or feelings of pity. We still look with pity upon the victims. However, we respond with gratitude that it is not ourselves or our families who are suffering. While we do not work on behalf of others, we use our limited feelings of pity to prevent these abuses of power from happening within our families. In a strange way, we are satisfied that we are combating evil by preventing it within our own communities while we abandon those on the outside.

The final marker of suffering/evil within our society is our bondage to evil. The Christian community has agreed for centuries that every action and every desire is disfigured. Every attempt on our part has been influenced by deception and callousness. The reality of human life is that we are trapped by the lies that we use to protect ourselves. Through these lies, we perpetrate evil against the many victims in the world.

But our bondage is not just an effect that we exert on the victims in our world. Our bondage to evil moves inward, damaging us. Even when we are not the victims of a particular event of evil, we are victims. Our humanness—our desire for justice, compassion, and love—is impaired and limited. As Wendy Farley describes the effect, "Sin becomes a kind of bondage that entangles human beings and communities even before they choose or desire evil."[9]

The effects of our bondage feed backward to the other markers of evil. The more we rely upon self-deception and callousness to inform and shape our world, the tighter the bonds of sin upon our lives. We travel farther and farther away from the real world and tie ourselves more closely to the delusional world of our own creation. There are many effects of all three markers, but they combine at one point. Over time we lose the language, the words that can break into our self-deceptive, callous, and sin-bound existence.

Suffering/evil is at once something that humanity inflicts on each other and the experience that we all share. We are both its victims and perpetrators. No one is completely pure or innocent of participating in the markers of evil. At the same time, no one is safe from being the object of evil and experiencing suffering. The bottom line is that all humans have

---

9. Farley, *Tragic Vision*, 49.

lost the ability to shape and form the words and carry out the actions that would make our existence authentic and just.

Suffering/evil has tricked us into believing that the world is evil and that there are no good people, nor are there any worthy actions. Each day we hear of stories of heroes fallen from grace. In this time it is steroid usage among Olympic athletes. In other ages it has been gambling or physical violence among political icons or film stars. Suffering/evil has contributed to our cynical view of the value of all human actions. We believe the worst of each other and have lost hope for the best.

In spite of this dreary outlook on civilization, we continue to long for the best, the brightest, and the beautiful. We seek grace and wonder in nature, art, music, and humanity. These are the characteristics that make us human. These are the gifts that God gives to us in our creation. The question becomes, can we fight back? Can we participate with each other and with God to stop the metastasizing effects of suffering/evil?

QUESTIONS FOR CONSIDERATION AND DISCUSSION

The questions are offered for your personal or group consideration. Consider answering them from personal experience. However, it is equally important to try to answer them from the perspective of a victim of suffering. Using a story of a current event of personal or community suffering, put yourself in the role of one of the people identified in the story. Now, using your understanding from the chapter, answer the questions from the view of that individual.

1. After reflecting on the chapter, have you ever experienced an impact upon your life that you would call suffering/evil?
2. What was the youngest age that you recall an experience that you would describe as suffering/evil?
3. How have you become aware of the power of certain events to reshape the way that you see others and the world?
4. How has suffering/evil reshaped your view of others and your view of the world?
5. What changes did this experience of suffering/evil make in the way that you act around other people and in the world?
6. What answers did other people offer to you about the source or cause of suffering?
7. Which of the markers of evil is most familiar to you?
8. In an occasion where you have misused your freedom and it has had the potential of injuring another, which of the markers did you employ to justify your actions?
9. Can you identify or recount attempts to fight back or resist the effects of anguish-suffering?
10. How would you describe God's role in the experience of suffering?

2

What Does God Have to Do with This?

To this point, you might have noticed a lack of comment about the role or influence of God in all this discussion of suffering. There is a very good reason for this. For much of Christian history, when suffering is discussed, the first attempt by Christians is to protect God. Protecting God might seem like an odd activity, but most people of faith do it at some time. It is natural that Christians and Jews would step forward in defense of God. Humans defend that which they love and which they believe loves them first or in return. That is how people of faith see God. God loves humanity and creation first as well as in response to human faithfulness.

This defense of God is grounded in three areas or assumptions about the human/divine relationship. First, faithful people defend what they trust to be true about the nature of God. Second, they defend God because it is a part of the responsibility to make disciples of others. Finally, they defend God because they believe they cannot fully understand God and therefore must defend the incomprehensible.

It seems logical and a sign of faithfulness to defend before all attackers that the nature of God is plain for all to see. Generations of believers have learned that the scriptures describe the nature of God as good, loving, and compassionate. People respond loudly and with great emphasis to charges against God because they are a painful insult to our faith. So we create explanations intended to keep victims of suffering/evil from blaming God.

DEFENDING GOD

People of faith are confident in the truth of God's loving nature. This confidence begins with the first words of the creation story as recorded in Genesis. God saw that God's creation was good, and God blessed the creation. The voice of the psalmist echoes the affirmation that God is good and loving. There are several different kinds of songs of praise in the collection of writings called the Psalms. We can look at examples from two different categories and see the confidence that humanity places in the goodness of God. First, there is Psalm 36, which is a psalm of praise. Verse 5 exults, "Your steadfast love, O Lord, extends to the heavens, your faithfulness to the clouds." The affirmation of God continues in verse 7, "How precious is your steadfast love, O God!"

The confidence that God's nature is love is also found in the psalms of lamentation. At the time of greatest destruction and pain, as the people of Israel are being enslaved by foreign powers, they affirm that the nature of God is love and compassion. In the group of songs numbered 137–139 in the Christian Bible, the words affirm that God knows the sufferer intimately. Psalm 138:7–8 affirms that belief in God is steadfast in love.

> Though I walk in the midst of trouble,
> you preserve me against the wrath of my enemies;
> you stretch out your and your right hand delivers me.
>
> The LORD will fulfill his purpose for me;
> your steadfast love, O LORD, endures forever,
> do not forsake the work of your hands.

This same affirmation echoes through the later writings of the Christian community. John wrote to the church in the city of Ephesus. His thoughts on the nature of God are preserved for us in the little letter of 1 John. The beautiful words of 1John 4 have strengthened the faith of Christians during times of joy and suffering, "God is love, and those who abide in love abide in God, and God abides in them" (1 John 4:16b).

These passages and many others help us to see that the first instinct to defend God is deeply rooted in knowledge of God as good and loving. The second reason for defending God is tied to the call of religion to evangelize or bring other people into the faith community. In Matthew 28:19, Jesus calls all believers to make disciples of all nations. The command comes from much earlier material. Through the prophet Jeremiah, God continually affirms that it is God's greatest desire that all people, all nations, come to know him. Jeremiah 23:3 reads:

What Does God Have to Do with This?

> Then I myself will gather the remnant of my flock out of the lands where I have driven them, and I will bring them back to their fold, and they shall be fruitful and multiply.

God's desire to gather all people to God's self is a foundational piece of the message of Jesus the Christ. As the gospel of John affirms in chapter 14, Jesus promises the disciples that there is room in God's eternal home for all children of God. In these chapters of the gospel, often called the Final Discourse, Jesus affirms that the nature of God is love, and God's loving nature desires the gathering of all creation into God's self.

The instinct to defend God becomes clearer as we understand the nature of God. It is difficult at best when we tell people that God is loving but sometimes sends pain and suffering for no apparent reason. Faithful people want others outside of the community to give God a chance to show God's loving, compassionate nature. So there must be another explanation for suffering. Otherwise, the task of believers to bring others to God in Jesus Christ cannot be accomplished.

Finally, we come to what might be the most honest reason for defending God. This is because of individual and communal humility. God is God. We know that. As our God, faithful people accept that God has the power and the right to do whatever God chooses within the creation. We therefore respond to criticisms of God with the affirmation that God acts in ways that are mysterious to humans.

The confusing and mysterious book of Job supports this defense among the faithful. The story is familiar to most, even if the biblical book has never been read. Job is a faithful man who was caught in a bet between God and Ha-satan (the Accuser). Ha-satan accused God of protecting Job from suffering, and therefore Job's love of God came not from faith but from gratitude for material possessions.

As the story unfolds, Job is stripped of everything: possessions, family, friends, and even his own health. The challenge remains: Where does Job's faithfulness lie? Is it rooted in his possessing many things, obvious signs of blessing by God, or with God's own self? The story ends with a conversation between Job and God. Job cries out for all who have suffered, "Why did this happen?" After God's extended answer, Job offers the final summary response:

> I know that you can do all things, and that no purpose of yours can be thwarted. . . . I have uttered what I did not understand, things

> too wonderful for me, which I did not know ... therefore I despise myself, and repent in dust and ashes (Job 42:2–6).

Of the three reasons behind the human instinct to defend God, this third may be the most powerful. In a spirit of honest and even depressing humility, humanity creates elaborate explanations for events of suffering because in the final tally, very little is understood about the divine power that creates, redeems, and sustains the creation each day.

These three paths of faith-based reasoning show that each day, each moment, people of faith fall into the trap of protecting God from the criticism that naturally arises out of suffering/evil. Even while we are repeating the age-old adages about pain and suffering, we must remember that God never asks us to defend God. Grounded in the knowledge that God does not need defending, the common proposals need examination if we are to break the cycle of damage that is inflicted upon a victim each time a well-meaning person of faith jumps to the defense of God.

From these common explanations has arisen a complicated structure in the discipline of theology. Theology comes from the Latin word *theologia* and means, "Words about God." This is the field of study of religious practice and experience. Through the field of theology, teachers of the church attempt to speak about God's relationship to the creation and the response of creation and offer direction for the faithful to grow toward God. Naturally, teachers since the very beginning of the Christian community have written about the question of suffering/evil.

A specialized area of teaching or instruction (often called a doctrine) has arisen in the search for answers. That doctrine is called theodicy. In the development of a doctrine about the source, cause, or reason for suffering/evil, Christians have gone to enormous intellectual effort to devise schemes where the blame for suffering does not fall upon God. Theodicy describes the arguments that attempt to show that God is righteous or just despite the experience of suffering/evil in the world. Theodicy arguments are a philosophical structure with three parts or steps. They work by trying to show that God is perfectly good and omnipotent despite the experiences of suffering in the world. All the proposals have serious weaknesses. While each is trying to reconcile the same dilemma, most often they succeed at the expense of human hope. This chapter will look at the most common answers to the theodicy challenge.

What Does God Have to Do with This?

THEODICY: THREE PROPOSALS

Long before the birth of Christ, the people of God in Judaism built their faith on the foundation of two statements about God. We have looked the first one already: God is good. The second is partnered with it: God is almighty or omnipotent. When trying to understand how there can be suffering in the world, one or both of these faith statements is challenged. For example, if God is all good or perfectly good, how can God allow suffering to exist? Is not suffering a direct contradiction to the nature of God? The second position is equally challenged. If God is almighty (omnipotent), how can suffering exist? Is there a reason that God in God's power cannot step in and stop the cause of suffering?

It is challenging to reconcile these two faith statements. In most occasions where we think we have come up with an answer, it works in just the immediate setting, such as suffering caused for example by a car accident. Parents might say to their teenagers, "It was God's plan that you should have this accident to teach you to drive with greater caution." While that sounds good in one setting, can the same reason be used for a family when an automobile accident results in the death of a parent? As the family weeps at the funeral, they will all be asking, "What is God's lesson now?"

What has proven impossible is to arrive at an explanation that works in all situations of suffering from the individual to the destruction of communities in horrors such as the Jewish Holocaust or the genocide in the Darfur region of Africa. Answers for individual situations seem trite and even cruel when applied to contexts of great human suffering/evil.

In attempts to find a solution, Christian and Jewish theologies have actually come up with several proposals. There are three explanations that, when used alone or in combination, try to account for the evil and extreme cruelty of society while protecting the nature and power of God. In a way, each proposal is attempting to examine the causes of suffering/evil from the side of God. They attempt to answer the question of what role suffering/evil plays within the purpose and work of a perfectly good and almighty God. The three proposals are that suffering/evil is:

1. Punishment for sin

2. One part of a greater plan (or the ultimate end of creation)

3. A method of education

A brief explanation of each position will reveal both its satisfying strength in the question of suffering as well as it weaknesses as it defends God.

Proposal 1: Suffering Is a Punishment for Sin

We have all heard this answer given at the times of painful events. Offered with humor or dead seriousness, the victim often asks, "What have I done to deserve this?" This most common proposal for the cause of suffering/evil at first encounter seems reasonable.

We even hear acceptance of this view in family and community conversation. In the moments following a tragedy when the question is asked, we look for answers. To the accident victim, we might point out a careless driving action by saying, "You do talk on your phone while driving."

The idea of suffering as a punishment for our sin is found grounded within the scriptures of the Jewish and Christian tradition. Any of the lament psalms help to reinforce this idea. We can read an example of this in Psalm 73, which leads us through this human process:

> Truly God is good to the upright,
>> To those who are pure in heart (73:1).
>
> For I was envious of the arrogant
>> I saw the prosperity of the wicked (73:3).
>
> Indeed, those who are far from you will perish;
>> You put an end to those who are false to you (73:27).

Haven't we all been in the place of the speaker of Psalm 73? We see people in our community, our family, or even our church prospering, and all the while we know that their family life is unhappy. Then a day comes when this success turns to ashes. The mighty and powerful are reduced to defending their lives in courts of law or courts of popular opinion. The righteous celebrate that God's justice has been served. The perpetrator of evil now suffers in punishment for his or her sin.

This first proposal, that suffering is the result of sin, is a satisfying answer until suffering visits our family, community, or home. Then the story is dramatically different. We can all tell this story because it is our suffering. A father dies and his family asks why they are left without the means to stay in their house, let alone pay for school, sports, or even college. Then we ask, what was his sin that he and his family should be punished in this way? Maybe the story is of a community that is devastated by a school shooting. This story is all too familiar in our society today. Whether we think of Colorado, Virginia, Ohio, or the streets of any city, when one innocent person dies, this proposal raises the question: who has sinned to such a degree to deserve the severity of this punishment? Could a teacher or student walking to class have made any better decisions that would have saved their lives?

The proposal that suffering is a punishment for sin sweeps the innocent into the mix with the guilty. As our world grows small through media and technology, we see the examples where this proposal punishes those who are really the victims of other's greed or misuse of power. The oppression of the innocent as well as the guilty is a problem with the second proposal for the source of suffering.

Proposal 2: Suffering/Evil Is One Part of God's Greater Plan.

The second theodicy proposal views suffering as just one part of the plan or great design that God holds for all creation. This proposal tells us that we experience suffering because we cannot know the mind and intent of God, nor can we see the entire plan. This position uses the cross of Christ as its symbolic source of meaning. Through the cross, the victim is to find consolation with assurances that God has a purpose that we cannot understand or judge. Just as Jesus pleaded with God to take the horror of the cross away, the sufferer can plead, all the while knowing that God's great plan will go forward to complete the loving purpose that God holds for the creation.

Some writers call this proposal the "too puny" defense. Addressing the sufferer, this proposal begins by offering words of consolation. The time-worn words, "God has a purpose that we cannot understand or that we cannot judge," slide through many conversations. Well-meaning friends, family, and even strangers on the news observe that we cannot know the reasons behind this tragedy. After a short time, the victims begin to repeat this message. The darkness of sorrow fills with despair and hopelessness. They are supposed to accept suffering with gratitude because God has a purpose.

Any pastor or rabbi can name people who fall into this category. We hear the news reports each year of college students who die in an accident while returning to campus after spring break. As we face the parents whose child has died, we seek to offer comfort and assurance with these words, "God has a plan." When a college student dies in a senseless accident where no one is at fault, the parents need to give meaning to the death of their child. Suffering from this perspective is God's effort to guide our choices and direct our lives away from human desires.

The comfort in this proposal comes in our confidence that God is truly omniscient or all-powerful. This confidence is expressed through two affirmations. The first is that God has a plan for cosmic order and justice. When suffering happens, we look signs of God's justice in action. We work to convince ourselves that God needs the life of a child in Minnesota to balance the evil found somewhere else in the world. The second affirmation is that God has a plan for each individual. Suffering comes to us as a sign that we have moved away from God's plan.

Faithful confidence in God's omniscience is crucial to the entire concept of God. The second proposal demonstrates God's all-encompassing knowledge while it shows the limitations of human knowledge. This proposal insists that all the victims of suffering/evil must accept everything that befalls them as somehow a necessary piece of God's eternal plan.

The Jewish people and all peoples who have undergone attempts of genocide can reveal the enormous problem with this view. The horror of the Holocaust defies any power in this proposal to explain suffering. How can humanity begin to accept suffering as a part of God's plan when we know the innocence of those who suffer? How could any plan of God's involve the sacrifice of God's blessed creatures?

Proposal 3: Suffering/Evil Is a Method of Education

The third proposal for the source or reason behind suffering/evil was made popular through the writings of C.S. Lewis during WWII. In his book, *The Problem of Pain*, Lewis advances the view that suffering is a tool used by God for the education of humanity. Sometimes this view is called suffering as pedagogy. This means that suffering has entered our lives so that we can learn from the experience.

This proposal is often confused in interpretation. Many people will say that they have learned something from their experiences of suffering. After a disabling illness or sudden loss, people will say that they learned to be more compassionate or to use their gifts more wisely. This is not the same as this third proposal. Suffering as pedagogy or suffering to educate says that God sends suffering for the purpose of teaching people a lesson.

Some have taught that the basic human inclination is to turn away from God. Because of this tendency, human existence is a constant struggle against those things that we would like to do and the will of God. Each moment humanity attempts to make choices between human desires and God's plan. At each wrong choice where we give into our own ego or lie to ourselves, pain will be the result.

Suffering in this proposal is God's effort to guide our choices and direct our lives away from selfish human desires. Each occasion where we refuse to yield ourselves to God, we will inevitably experience pain and suffering. According to Lewis, through the pain that accompanies suffering, God "shatters the creature's false sense of self-sufficiency."[1] Suffering and its accompanying pain becomes God's megaphone, "To rouse a deaf world."[2] For example the third-century preacher St. Augustine preached that suffering teaches us to ask God only for something that is good.[3]

Suffering as education is the proposal frequently heard in the church. Maybe for that reason it is the one that disturbs me the most. I recall two children who came into the emergency room when I was working as a student chaplain. Their parents brought them in accompanied by the police. It seems a kindly neighbor who had won the trust of the families was sexually abusing these two little girls. What lesson did these two little girls need to be taught by God? We can think of many other examples. What did the family have to learn when an intoxicated driver drove head-on into their automobile, killing the father and one of the children? Or the innocent tribal peoples of the Sudan or other war-torn areas of the world, what lessons did they need to learn?

ADDITION GETS YOU HEAVEN

Most people do not use any one of these proposals alone to explain the reason or purpose for suffering/evil. Many times pieces of each one are added together to create a fourth proposal that says that suffering is tied to an ultimate end. Suffering may come from sin or as a piece of God's

1. Lewis, *The Problem of Pain*, 101.
2. Lewis, 91.
3. Augustine, *The Works of St. Augustine*, 82.

plan or even to educate, but whatever the source, all suffering leads the faithful to the ultimate end of a reward in heaven. This reward is for those who suffer with patience the injustices of life. The promise is that God holds out a reward to the faithful, but first they must endure all kinds of pain and sorrow. "You have earned stars in your crown in heaven," is one version of the assurances offered to victims in an attempt to ease their suffering.

Religious leaders preach this combination of the three proposals. As pastors and rabbis seek to find their own meaning in suffering/evil, they use the promise of heaven as a carrot to dangle before the victims. They offer assurances that suffering will bring the reward of joy, and pain will resolve ultimately into perfect happiness. When the religious leader uses this premise, the suffering is often tied to a vow made before God. For example, an abused spouse might hear something like, "Stay for the sake of the children, or stay because of your vows before God, and God will bless you." Sufferers come to believe that if they step aside from the suffering, God will not forgive them and they will forfeit any promise of eternal salvation.

Each of these proposals, either individually or when added together, contains a kernel of truth. People of many faiths believe the premises behind each proposal. Sin or bad choices is an accepted characteristic of human existence. The mysterious and unknown nature of God is foundational in all religions. Finally, we accept the premise that all humanity needs to learn how to be better people. We all hope for and desire to win the promise of eternal life that is free of suffering a pain.

Sadly, all these proposals bring us to the same point. The sufferer sees no hope in the present and clings to the promise that at some point at the end of life, the suffering will come to a complete end. The loss of hope results from two profound effects that these proposals have upon all of us. First, these proposals teach us that the love and compassion of God comes to us as a reward. Second, these proposals leave us feeling hopeless because they reject the idea that there is value in our finite and earthly existence.

THE TRUTH ABOUT GOD

In the midst of suffering/evil, as we search for reasons, it is easy to forget two basic facts about the nature of God. First, people of faith must hold

What Does God Have to Do with This?

on to the promise that God does not withhold God's compassionate love until we learn enough to deserve it. Second, the omnipotent God does not use pain to teach us to be more obedient. God does not hold out the promise of heaven as a carrot to entice the faithful into willingness to suffer and endure oppression in this life. God does not demand that children or spouses stay and accept physical and emotional abuse so that they can one day attain eternal life.

Besides forgetting the basic nature of God, these proposals lead us to reject the idea that there is value in our earthly existence. It places life-now in competition with the promised life-to-come. Life-now is to be tolerated, but also it is to be rejected as inferior and corrupt. Certainly this view is a direct conflict with the life of Jesus the Christ. Jesus healed and relieved the pain of many so that life-now could be all that God intended.

It would seem from these four proposals that the God we call loving and just plans that all human life is shadowed with suffering and pain. They diminish the value that God placed upon humanity in creation. These four proposals dismiss all the scriptural promises that God loves and treasures the creation. Finally, they challenge the teaching that God chose to become human through the incarnation of Jesus.

We are quick to quote and believe any one or a combination of these four proposals. Christian communities, their members and their leaders, have convinced us that suffering is our fault and that there is no hope for us in this present life. We should gratefully endure the pain of oppression because God is either reshaping us in this life or offering heaven as a reward for all who can endure.

We never questioned these answers, as obscene and absurd as they sound. We accept them because they have been tied to the foundational teachings of our faith. We cling to the faith promise that God is all good and loving as well as omnipotent and consequently accept that somehow God has planned for us to suffer or alternatively, that God sends suffering into our lives.

How did we get here? How did the community of faith find itself at this point where defending our belief that God is loving and omnipotent means believing in a God who punishes us so horribly? These four proposals come to the faith community with a long history. Most believers are familiar with what is formally known as the Western theological tradition. These are the teachings that came into the Christian community from the great teachers in Europe. Before we can uncover other traditions about suffering, it is helpful to look at the tradition that is so ingrained into the Christian community that it has led us to the four proposals described above.

What Does God Have to Do with This?

QUESTIONS FOR CONSIDERATION AND DISCUSSION

1. Defending God is natural to people of faith. Which of the three assumptions was most familiar?
2. How would you describe the nature of God?
3. What does it mean to you to describe God as good? What synonyms come to mind?
4. What other terms do you use to describe God as omnipotent?
5. Give a concrete example of where someone has used each of the three proposals for the source of suffering as an explanation.

    a. Punishment for sin
    b. Part of a greater plan
    c. A method of education

6. How does the proposal of suffering as a punishment for sin differ from the explanation that each action in life holds consequences?
7. Do you believe that God's plan is hidden from us, or is it revealed in any way?
8. The college student dies in a car accident during the return to campus from spring break. Accepting the proposal that God is using pain as a means of education, how can you help these parents understand the death of their child?
9. How is suffering sent by God as education different that saying, "I have experienced pain and have learned something from it"?
10. A woman comes to you having recently miscarried what would have been her second child. She shares that at eighteen she had an abortion and asks you to explain God's role in her recent loss. What do you say?

3

Scripture and Tradition: What Does the Bible Say?

THE JOURNEY TO UNDERSTAND the place and meaning of suffering/evil begins by delving into God's word. While there are many biblical passages that have influenced understanding about suffering and its relationship to God, two hold the greatest influence. The first are the creation stories recorded in the book of Genesis. The second source of biblical material is found in the writings of St. Paul, particularly the book of Romans.

For many generations readers have assumed that in reading these passages there is very little question about the nature of God. As mentioned in the first chapter, the authors of scripture are confident that God is compassionate, righteous, omnipotent, and perfectly good. Their confidence is built upon the promises found in all of scripture combined with the ongoing experience of the faithful.

As generations of scholars have studied the scriptures to unlock the true nature of God, they have also searched these passages to come to an understanding of the nature of humanity. Using Genesis 1:26 and following, they have built the case that the nature of humanity is intimately tied to the nature of God through creation. Following this thinking, suffering/evil are then as a consequence intimately tied to the relationship between God and humanity. Humanity created in the image of God seeks to know God through an ongoing examination of human strengths and flaws.

Genesis 1 begins a story that is familiar to most believers. It is common knowledge that God created the universe, accomplishing this event in just seven days! The faith community faces two challenges as we reflect on the record of God's acts in creation. The first challenge is to pay careful attention to what is actually recorded in the first chapter of the book of Genesis. Too often the record of the creation of humanity in Genesis 1:26–28 is given little consideration. The Christian community has acted

Scripture and Tradition: What Does the Bible Say?

as if the real story or more accurate version is recorded in Genesis 2:4b and following.

The second challenge is that we cannot read this passage without the influence of generations of interpretations. Our understanding of the meaning of the text has already been influenced or biased by what we have been taught through Sunday school, sermons, or Bible studies. We have all heard the sermons that blamed the woman for all suffering or the ones that tell us of God's anger.

The beginning point for this chapter is to read the passage as printed below and enter into a consideration of its meaning:

> Then God said, "Let us make humankind in our image, according to our likeness; and let them have dominion over the fish of the sea, and over the birds of the air, over the cattle, and over all the wild animals of the earth, and over every creeping thing that creeps upon the earth." So God created humankind in his image, in the image of God he created them; male and female he created them. God blessed them and God said to them, "Be fruitful and multiply, and fill the earth and subdue it; and have dominion over the fish of the sea and over the birds of the air and over every living creature that moves upon the earth (Gen 1:26-28).

To understand the place of this passage in the study of suffering/evil is to ask the first the question of why this passage was written. Scholars tell us that it is not meant to be a statement of scientific discovery or medical fact. Nor is it meant to be an abstract statement about the origins of the cosmos. The record of Genesis 1—2:4a was written to be used in worship and praise of God by God's chosen people when they were being oppressed in exile in Babylon. For thousands of years, when people of faith read and recited this passage, they were affirming that their faith was grounded in God, who is the creator of all there is.

So, from the beginning, the record of Genesis is about God and God's nature. The beginning encounter with the text of Genesis affirms three dominant ideas for the people of faith. First, God creates through God's power that exceeds all other forms of power. Second, God loves and delights in the creation. Finally, God blesses the creation by calling it good.

As a prerequisite to understanding the question of suffering and finding hope in creation, we must constantly remind ourselves that God is more powerful than anything else in creation. Too often in the face of great evil we fall into the trap of accepting the human judgment that a particularly tragic event was too great even for God to stop it from happening. In the twenty-first century, citizens of the United States are tempted to apply this assumption to the events that resulted in the destruction of the World Trade Center. In a similar manner, theologians ponder the power of evil verses the power of God in the vicious destruction of innocent people in the European holocaust. We must be wary of assigning power to evil and suffering at the expense of diminishing what we believe to be the power of God.

When we are in the midst of suffering, it is difficult to accept or to prove that God loves and delights in humanity. We are much more likely to search for the human/personal flaw that has motivated God to turn from us. The scriptural record is clear: God returns again and again to reestablish a relationship with humanity because God loves humanity. In the pages ahead, we will return to this theme.

Finally, in affirming the foundational assumptions about God, we must recall that God calls the creation good. This is a word of blessing as it is recorded in Genesis 1. Wendy Farley, at the very end of her work, *Tragic Vision and Divine Compassion,* writes, "Evil is stronger than good; struggles for justice and redemption cannot hope to overcome either the tragic structures of creation or the historical realities of selfishness and violence."[1] As I have read and reread Farley's final assessments, I continue to disagree. God is the source of all good in the creation. Even though humanity too often perverts or attempts to damage God's good, it is stronger than the evil that humanity generates.

THINKING ABOUT GENESIS 1

There will always be more to be learned about the entire record of creation, and the reading list at the end of the book identifies resources where the reader can continue this study. For the purposes of this chapter, the specific verses of Genesis 1:26–28 will be the focus. There are four primary actions of God recorded in this account. First, God creates humanity in God's image as well as in God's likeness. The Hebrew shows that these are two different characteristics of God's creation of humanity.

---

1. Farley, *Tragic Vision,* 131.

In the second primary action, God creates humanity with the separate sexual identities of male and female. It is clear that sexual identity belongs to the creation and not to God. God, unlike the created human, is neither male nor female. It is also clear that God celebrates the sexual identity of humanity; after all, it was God's idea.

The third action is that God charges the humans with the care of the creation. The word used is often "dominion" or "rule." The charge is not to use the creation to satisfy human desires. The command is to govern the creation as God governs, through love and compassion. By example, God gives of God's self to create humanity therefore humanity must give of themselves to see that creation becomes all that God intended for it to be.

The fourth action that is highlighted from the text is the choice that God makes by blessing humanity. When God calls human creation good, it is not a description of the moral quality of men and women. This is not a record of a humanity that is at this moment perfect. Rather, God is describing the Creator's response to the human creation. God finds humanity to be pleasing and beautiful. At these final words of the passage, the divine creator affirms that human creation along with all of creation is now the place where God will continuously dwell, bringing God's gifts of love and freedom.

While Genesis 1:1–28 sets the stage for God's relationship to creation, it is not the first passage often considered when the question of suffering/evil is raised. To confront the painful teachings of the church about suffering/evil, careful consideration must be directed to the following longer passage in Genesis that begins with Genesis 2:4b.

Genesis 2:4b begins the intense continuation of the creation story that was gathered into the record by faithful people. Here the reader is painfully challenged by the teachings and instructions of the church. Generations of teachings about sin or evil cloud the word of God conveyed through this text. As in all good Bible study, the first question is, "What exactly is found in this text, and what is not there at all?"

In answer to this question, careful reading reveals that there are three insights that this text shares. Chapter 2 reveals that God calls humanity. Then God grants permission to humanity to work in the creation. Finally, God demonstrates that calling and permission come with responsibility and prohibitions. These insights are the foundation for reading what follows in chapter 3.

The reader must remember that these passages were recorded to give the faithful additional insight into the nature of God. In 2:4b–17 the careful reader learns that God is the creator of all, having made a creature from clay that was totally dependent upon God. First, this creature was given the calling or vocation by God to tend to the needs of the garden. Within the Christian community, calling or vocation is recognized as a gift from God. God has gifted each individual with specific talents and abilities that the human is to use in praise of God.

In many places in the New Testament, there are partial lists of gifts, such as the one found in Ephesians 4:11. These lists point our attention away from our human desires for fame or fortune by directing us back to the purpose of the gifts. As recorded in Genesis 2, each gift given by God is for the purpose of building up the body of the believers (Eph 4:12) through following the way of the love and compassion of God as known through Jesus the Christ (1 Cor 12:31).

The second insight the reader takes from the passage is that this gift of life and calling is empowered by God's permission to use the garden to ensure life. God expects humanity to be engaged in the creation. It is there for nourishment and refreshment. Life is not just about gaining possessions or dominating the world around us. Life, as God intends, is arriving at the delicate balance of meeting our human needs of sustenance that are both physical and spiritual. Humanity can certainly take its needs from the creation but also must return to the creation the care that it needs to continue in existence.

Finally, the third insight is that calling and permission carry with them the responsibility of prohibition. The human, dependent upon God, must follow God's instructions, because these instructions will ensure the continuation of creation as God has created. The subject of prohibition is something that humanity likes to avoid. The passage does not say that to this point humanity is perfect. In fact, the clear presence of this limiting word suggests that God, at the beginning of creation, recognizes that imperfect humanity needs restrictions or there will be catastrophic results.

All of these crucial ideas are packed into Genesis 2:4b–17. The record of God's plan intensifies with the creation of the helpmate. The creation is dependent upon the guidance and care of humanity, and God creates a partnership to share in the responsibilities of loving the creation. In the garden, God has created a community between God, humanity, and the

Scripture and Tradition: What Does the Bible Say?

creation. It is God's plan that this community be grounded in love, trust, and solidarity between all.

The next section in this critical story from Genesis is one filled with difficulties. There is the record of the serpent. Christian tradition has given the serpent a variety of powers and characteristics. One interpretation is that the serpent represents evil entering the creation. There is no support for this claim in the text. The Word in Genesis uses a device called serpent to give voice to the human weakness of taking clearly given prohibitions and turning them into options to be evaluated through free choice. The serpent represents humanity's turning from the love of God to the love of self and selfish desires.

Scripture does not call the serpent evil. The term used is sly or subtle. The serpent represents the streetwise wisdom of humanity that we like to pretend does not exist until we need to outwit a boss or spouse or child.[2] Neither Adam nor Eve delays their actions until they can have a consultation with their creator. They seem to have dismissed the fact that God will walk with them again at evening and they could confer with God about the words of the serpent and the prohibition.

The effect of sly wisdom is to show that God can be excluded from human decisions. Human anxiety about choice and knowledge plays out in dismissal of God's love and plan for the safety of humanity. The remainder of the scriptural story shows that excluding God leads to disastrous results.

Our understanding of what follows in Genesis 3 has been tainted by generations of Christian interpretation. Even our printed Bibles lead us away from the point of the story. In some Bibles, Genesis 3:8 and following is titled "The Judgment of God." This title is not in scripture. It is the addition and interpretation of the translators and editors who assembled these versions of the Bible. Students of scripture cannot be distracted by these inserted interpretations.

Rather than reading Genesis 3 as the record of God's punishment, faithful students read these passages as a miracle of God's intervention into creation. Genesis 2 sets the stage as it teaches that dismissing and disobeying God's word results in death. In Genesis 3, God reveals that God does not allow the humankind to die. Rather than death, the creator God of love chooses life for humankind.

---

2. Bellis, *Helpmates, Harlots, and Heroes*, 56.

The promise of new life meets and reaffirms the faith-forming purpose of the first three chapters of Genesis. The record affirms that God is the creator who loves the creation without reserve. God has a plan for the creation to remain in relationship to the creator throughout life. Finally, God, when faced with human anxiety, devious behavior, and disobedience, does the most surprising thing. God's grace works out a path for life to continue, though with more difficulty than before. In other words, even when humans ignore God, rejecting the call to trust, God reconciles creation to God's self through compassionate love. This is the human/divine relationship that carries through generations of creation.

However, knowing that God is constant in love and compassion has not stopped the experience of suffering/evil. It continues to be a constant companion to humanity. Generations of believers struggle through the challenge of finding meaning or understanding when pain and tragedy enter our personal lives or the lives of friends and families.

In this search, people of faith continue to interpret Genesis using other passages in the scriptures. They seek to reaffirm the promises by finding "other places" where God says the same thing. Human insecurity keeps us from believing God's first words unless we can find them repeated again and again in other places. The psalms that are songs of praise and lament are a powerful place to gain understanding about God's sustaining love for the creation. In addition, Christians have often used Paul's letter to the church at Rome to provide understanding. Despite all the assurances and reassurances of God's gracious, compassionate, loving nature, the questions have lingered. Why does suffering happen, and what is the relationship between God, humanity, and suffering?

In an attempt to find a rational answer, the passage found in Romans 5:12–14 has been frequently cited as an explanation. This passage is quite familiar and is frequently found within forms of confession within Christian communities. Paul writes:

> Therefore, just as sin came into the world through one man and death came through sin, and so death spread to all because all have sinned (Rom 5:12).

The place to begin is with questions addressed to the text. What does it really say, and is Paul correct in his interpretation of the Genesis story? First, we must remember that Paul is a product of his own education and experience. Paul was educated within the Jewish community to serve as a legal expert. It is of course within the characteristics of the law that one seeks logical and human answers to all issues. So Paul, seeking an explanation for the suffering experienced by humanity, repeats what he has learned. Suffering comes from God, and it is God's response to the disobedience of humanity.

As we read it above, it clearly says that death spread throughout all people because all people have sinned. This means that all humanity is born with sin that will taint, if not despoil, all thoughts, actions, and intentions of humanity singly or in community. The first humans, Adam and Eve, predetermined all these actions that led to suffering. In fact, Paul is certain that the woman, Eve, has greater responsibility for the presence of suffering/evil within the world than the male, Adam.

Built on this understanding of inherited sin, this fallen nature of humanity renders humanity enemies of God and condemns humanity to a pain-filled life. In relationship to suffering, this English translation of Romans would assure us that humanity is the cause and source of all suffering, pain, and by extension all evil in the world. The cause is rooted in the evil nature of humanity and the inability of humanity to resist evil actions and thoughts.

Paul's teaching in Romans seems to be affirmed in two other passages found in the New Testament. In 1 Corinthians 15:43, a passage addressing the resurrection, Paul describes the human as one "sown in dishonor." Using the verse from Romans as guide to interpretation, Paul is clear. The perishable, finite human cannot attain salvation. In addition, the perishable, finite human cannot even contain the divine. In other words, nothing that humans do will correct or fix the broken relationship between humanity and God. On top of that, humanity is so damaged that God can no longer work through humanity to attain God's goals.

This position seems to be affirmed by another passage in 1 Timothy. First, we must recognize that Paul probably did not write this book. However, its author is applying Paul's teaching to the church. As suffering continued to punish the faithful members of the church, teachers sought answers just as we do today. The author of Timothy provides an answer by narrowing the sin of humanity to the person of Eve. The author absolves Adam of any participation in the actions that have led the world into sin as he wrote:

> For Adam was formed first, then Eve; and Adam was not deceived, but the woman was deceived and became a transgressor (1 Tim 2:13–14).

From this passage, believers are taught that all the sin and suffering of the world and the condition of original sin are the fault of Eve, the woman that God created.

Very practical concerns in the growing young church led to the adding of these three passages together and resulted in the doctrine of original sin. In the first two hundred years of the church, the practice was to baptize new believers soon after their conversion to Christianity. Eventually a church teacher asked the simple question of why. What is it about the nature of humanity that as soon as possible humanity must be baptized to be found acceptable by God? The answer came from the Augustine of Hippo. His view ultimately became the primary interpretation for the church.

In the fourth century, this great teacher of the church wrote about the nature of human life. Interpreting the text of Genesis, Augustine describes humanity as fallen. In this term, Augustine was following the thinking that humanity was once pristine and now has lapsed. On the one hand, this theological position means that humanity cannot return to God from any of its own action that sets the stage for the Christ. On the other hand, this position means that humanity is so fallen that they cannot make any contribution to God's plan for salvation of the creation.

Augustine's teachings began the journey of moving away from the content of Genesis and into the interpretation of the scripture. Recall from Chapter Two that the word of God in Genesis never describes humanity as perfect. However, Augustine, in his teaching and interpretation, moved beyond Genesis. He continued by placing the foundation of his teaching in Paul's letter to Rome where the focus is on the fallen state of humanity.

Paul influenced Augustine through his writings in Romans that through Adam sin has entered the world. The object of Paul's writings is the human desire to cling to human laws as the norm for existence. Paul writes to refocus this energy in the correct direction of the salvation to be found in Christ, demonstrating the difference between Christ and humanity. As the story of Christ unfolds, leading to the crucifixion, many generations of teachers have drawn the conclusion that the inherent nature of humanity is evil.

Teachings in the Christian community growing out of the writings of Augustine describe human life as a tragic story of pain, suffering, and evil. The long-term effect has been to see the actions of Adam and Eve as the revolt of all that is evil in direct opposition to the all-goodness of God. With regard to suffering/evil, according to the teachings of Augustine, the sin of Adam (turning from God) "defiles all humanity including children, who have no sins of their own. Therefore, all human beings are condemned because of the sin of Adam."[3] Ultimately Augustine arrived at the conclusion that human nature has no power to contribute good actions to God's plan of salvation.

Many generations later, modern writers such as Douglas John Hall, echoing the themes from Augustine, describe humanity as full of ambiguity, duplicity, and life moving toward death.[4] Utilizing Paul's descriptions of the purpose and work of Jesus Christ, Hall writes, "Biblical faith does not flinch or cloak in pretty phrases its assumption that being human means suffering."[5] While it is impossible to disagree, there is a serious question about the balance of the image presented within the scriptures. Where is the compassionate God who desires justice for the creation? Where is the loving God?

Centuries of theological writing beginning with Augustine concretized Paul's view into the "correct" view. In his sermons on Romans, Augustine establishes the interpretation that the fall means that humanity is diseased, with no hope in this life.[6] Augustine writes, "This is the battle of the saints: and in this warfare you are always at risk, until you die."[7] Hall pragmatically accepts the divide between humanity and Christ. Then he attempts to soften the Augustinian position by making a distinction between suffering that, as a result of the fall, is a part of the human drama and suffering that he calls the great burden of humanity.[8] While this distinction is intended to offer comfort, it leads further into the abyss

---

3. Papageorgiou, "Chrysostom and Augustine," 361–78.
4. Hall, *God and Human Suffering*, 128.
5. Hall, 32.
6. Augustine, *Sermons*, 36.
7. Augustine, 72.
8. Hall, 74.

where the value of life is found in the degree and nature of suffering/evil. Experiences of pain, fear, and loss will lead the faithful closer to God and into God's eternal kingdom. This is accomplished through the central point of God's plan: the crucifixion of Christ.

Interpretation of Genesis and New Testament writings through the view of Augustine has two horrific results. First, all suffering and all evil is blamed upon humanity. The extreme nature of the disease within humanity can lead only to the conclusion that humanity brings upon itself all the suffering. The situation actually goes one step further in that the extreme suffering experienced by humanity is actually nothing more than what humans deserve.

Augustine's position also affects the faith claims of Christianity in two ways. First, God cannot be omnipotent. God created a system where a once-perfect being became infected with a disease that will destroy all generations. This destructive disease will lead to the horrifying necessity of God sacrificing God's own son. How could this be the result of an all-powerful God who controls and directs the creation?

Second, there is no hope for humanity in this system. Hope is the faith in things promised by God, such as justice and compassion. Flawed humanity cannot ever see God's plan, let alone work out any portion of it within the creation. Humanity is condemned to the repetitious cycle of evil and suffering until the point where God ends all time. Popular interpretations of this event stress the cataclysmic view of wars without end and generations of humanity suffering in untold numbers.

The combination of these two positions results in the theological dilemma of theodicy that can only be resolved when either God's goodness or power have been diminished or humanity is reduced to a hopeless existence. In any case, in the present life, humanity sees God as either disinterested in human suffering or the source of the suffering. Only in eternity is this breach between God and humanity resolved.

In a brief review, the four proposals for the cause and meaning in suffering/evil fail to lead humanity into the hope of God. In fact, the traditional interpretation of the foundational scripture and subsequent tradition contribute to diminishing the power of God in two stages. As we look to renew the construction that we bring meaning to suffering, we must return to the beginning.

Constructing a response to suffering returns to questions about God. Genesis 1 offers answers to questions of "Who is God and what is

Scripture and Tradition: What Does the Bible Say?

God's plan?" However, understanding something more about God is not enough. The second question is about humanity, "What does it mean to be created in the image and likeness of God?" Understanding the relationship of humanity to God will not on its own bring hope to the sufferers. The final question asks about the purpose and work of Christ. Genesis 1 can help the sufferer understand the plan of God to redeem the creation that begins in Genesis and continues through God becoming human as a baby at Bethlehem.

QUESTIONS FOR CONSIDERATION AND DISCUSSION

1. In times of pain or sorrow, what is your favorite passage from scripture? What meaning does it bring to you?

2. Are you more familiar with one creation story than the other? Does it matter?

3. As you have learned through the Christian community, what is the role of the man and the woman in the creation story? How is that the same or different than the view in the chapter?

4. Wendy Farley wrote, "Evil is stronger than good; struggles for justice and redemption cannot hope to overcome either the tragic structures of creation or the historical realities of selfishness and violence."[9] What is your response to Farley's position?

5. How do the three insights affect the way that you view your own life, especially in the experience of suffering?

6. What is your response to the explanation of the serpent?

7. With all the suffering in the world, reflect on the ability of humanity to contribute good actions to God's plan of salvation.

8. How would you describe your idea of the "correct view" of the human life? Is suffering/evil predetermined? Can suffering/evil be thwarted?

9. How do you define hope? What does it mean to you to find hope in the times of suffering/evil or within the experience of anguish?

10. In preparation for Chapter Four, how do you describe God's plan for creation?

---

9. Farley, *Tragic Vision*, 131.

4

Becoming: God's Goal for the Creation

GENESIS 1–3 IS THE record of God's people as they attempt to answer humanity's cry of "Where is God in our time of suffering?" When faithful people wrote the words of Genesis, suffering had come through exile in a foreign land. History and scripture tell us that the chosen people had been enslaved through two violent events. The first of these events occurred around 721 BCE,[1] when invaders destroyed the Northern Kingdom of Israel. The Assyrian armies took many of the people into exile, leaving destruction behind. Again in the 500s BCE, the Southern Kingdom of Judah was destroyed. At this time, the Babylonians leveled the city of Jerusalem and its temple and took the people into captivity. The cries to God over these two catastrophic events happening in the history of one people sound through the scriptures. We read the words of despair, anger, and hopelessness in the prophets, such as Isaiah and Jeremiah, who lived through these events.

For faithful people through many generations, suffering/evil has taken every form conceived by the darkest depths of the human imagination. In all forms, suffering/evil has tried to destroy lives through religious oppression, political destruction, and deprivation of food, health, and other basic necessities. It does not matter if they are victims of psychological or physical abuse, individuals, or entire nations; victims cry, "Where is God?"

We all know that the cry is not new. We can trace the ongoing struggle to find an answer from the time of Paul to teachers of the church. However, all answers have not been the same. Recall the three answers supplied by the community of faith. Each in its own way replies that God is busy sending suffering. It says that suffering is God's way to educate humanity, inflict punishment for sin, or is just an unknowable part of God's

1. Note: BCE stands for Before the Common Era.

greater plan. Chapter Three outlined how all of these answers alone or combined have led and continue to lead people away from hope and into deeper despair. How can a child with leukemia hope for recovery when it seems that God has "sent" the disease for divine reasons? Thankfully these are not the only theological answers that the Christian community has found through prayer and the study of scripture.

To find a theological answer that brings hope to the sufferer, attention must be given to the teachers revered by Eastern Orthodox Christianity. Some of these teachers wrote far less than later teachers like Augustine. However, they demonstrate to us that Augustine's view of humanity was not and is not the only description within the Christian community. They teach that there is not just one answer to the meaning of suffering. If Augustine's heritage leaves sufferers with little or no hope, these teachers see great hope in God's oneness of self and singleness of purpose. God created for the sole purpose of being in communion, perfect relationship, with creation. Suffering/evil damages that relationship, and hope in God will bring us the only answer to the question, "Where is God?"

One such teacher of the early church is Irenaeus of Lyon. Today Irenaeus is recognized as a great teacher from the second century. He was in the first generation of teachers and thinkers of the young Christian church following the generation of the apostles. Born about 130 CE[2] of a Christian family, Irenaeus studied with and read the reflections of the first generation of teachers, including the gospels and letters of Paul. It is believed that he was sent by the church in Smyrna in Asia Minor (now Izmir, Turkey) to evangelize the community in Gaul called Lyon. He had been assigned the title of bishop, which in the second century was used to designate a teacher of some authority who carried particular responsibilities for the founding of a church. So in the second century, Irenaeus was a Christian missionary sent to the western reaches of the Roman Empire.

Being a Christian had never been without peril since the time of the writing of the gospels. In the gospel of Luke, one can read about the threats of death and assault that were aimed at Christians. For example, we read in Luke 21:12 where Jesus warns the disciples:

> But before all this occurs, they will arrest you and persecute you; they will hand you over to synagogues and prisons, and you will be brought before kings and governors because of my name.

2. Note: CE is used to denote the Common Era. Formerly AD was used for this designation.

These attacks escalated during the persecution of Marcus Aurelius, the Roman Emperor from CE 161–180. Irenaeus saw the effects that these sufferings had upon the faith of the Christian community.

As the cry for God's presence was raised in response to attacks from outside the Christian community, Irenaeus was also alarmed by dangerous teachings within the Christian community. It seemed that it was not enough suffering that the Christian community was under attack by the armies of the Roman emperor. The faithful were also under attack from teachers who were drawing people away from scripture and Christ with teachings that Irenaeus and others identified as heretical.

In response to both types of assault, internal and external, Irenaeus turned to the scriptures. He began his study with the record of God's creation of humanity in Genesis 1:26–28a.[3] In the record of Genesis, Irenaeus understood that the heart of humanity is found in its service of God, the creator. God and creation are inexorably tied together. For Irenaeus, any answer or direction found in the face of suffering was grounded in God's relationship to the creation. We can arrange his proposals into three steps that are the response when the sufferer asks, "Where is God?" These three steps are directly related to God the creator, humanity the creature, and Christ the Redeemer.

In the first step, Irenaeus answered that God the creator of all is always working to bring reconciliation back into the created order. In the second step, Irenaeus focused on the nature of humanity. He turned again to Genesis 1:26 to describe humanity as participants in God's plan. Finally, in the third step, Irenaeus drew out the true location of hope. He demonstrated that it is the power of God becoming human—Jesus Christ—that brings hope through resistance to suffering.

STEP ONE: GOD AND CREATION

Irenaeus was filled with theological awe as well as spiritual devotion to the understanding that God is the creator of all. This is the first and greatest of the subjects that he challenged others to accept. As he wrote:

---

3. Then God said, "Let us make humankind in our image, according to our likeness; and let them have dominion over the fish of the sea, over the birds of the air, and over the cattle, and over all the wild animals of the earth, and over every creeping thing that creeps upon the earth." So God created humankind in his image, in the image of God he created them; male and female he created them. God blessed them.

> It is proper, then, that I should begin with the first and most important head, that is, God the Creator, who made the heaven and the earth, and all things that are therein (whom these men blasphemously style the fruit of a defect), and to demonstrate that there is nothing either above Him or after Him; nor that, influenced by any one, but of His own free will, He created all things, since He is the only God, the only Lord, the only Creator, the only Father, alone containing all things, and Himself commanding all things into existence.[4]

With this devotion to God's self-appointed place as creator, it is understandable that to find an answer to the questions of suffering/evil, God's relationship to the creation is the crucial starting point. If Irenaeus were to offer a short answer to the question, "Where is God at the time of suffering/evil?" he would say, "Actively working in creation!" In the act of creating, Irenaeus identified God's plan to reconcile creation. What is God doing during this work? God is working with humanity to fulfill God's plan to reconcile all creation to God's self. The long answer will fill in the details.

To begin with, it is important to note that Irenaeus read the passages of Genesis 1–3 in a way that was far more modern than other teachers of his time, such as Augustine. Rather than use the abstract categories of Greek philosophy to interpret scripture, Irenaeus relied upon good sense and his love of concrete facts. While he recognized that the creation story is symbolic, carrying a special meaning for the believers, Irenaeus saw it as the voice of the omnipotent and creative God.[5] As he listened to the voice of God through the passage of Genesis 1:26–28, Irenaeus described three aspects of these passages that are critical to our understanding of God's plan for reconciliation.

First, through the creation story believers learn that God has and is creating an open universe of all that is known to God. As Irenaeus writes, "Not one of the things which have been, or are, or shall be made escapes the knowledge of God."[6] Second, within God's plan there is a unity between God and the creation. The power of God for hope and compassion comes through this unity. This unity is the sign of God's plan to allow a new beginning within creation where humanity can be restored to God.

---

4. Irenaeus, *Against Heresies*, Book II.1.1.
5. Lawson, *The Biblical Theology of Saint Irenaeus*, 118.
6. Irenaeus, *Against Heresies*, Book II.26.3.

Becoming: God's Goal for the Creation

Restoration is the third aspect of God's plan and begins with God's incarnation in Jesus the Christ. Irenaeus calls this action recapitulation.

The concept of an open universe is often a difficult one to grasp. Possibly it is better to think of this in terms of an open future. From the very first centuries of Judaism and into the formation of Christianity, God's promise of a future echoes. This future comes to completeness when God's kingdom of peace and justice is inaugurated. This view of the future, built upon prophetic promises, sees the future of humanity "as an open field of human hope and responsibility."[7]

First, the open or prophetic view of the universe rejects the idea that there is a specific, predetermined ending for people or for the creation. In other words, the open view rejects the idea that, for example, the completely grown oak tree is already contained within an acorn. It also rejects the idea that humanity is inherently either good or evil. For example, as a young couple gazes at the face of their newborn, they see all possibilities open before the child. The diagnosis of Down Syndrome does not seal the future. It only contributes to the possibilities.

God's creation of an open universe relies upon and expects that humanity will play a part in the shaping of the future. As the child grows, everyone who touches her life has a choice. Will they leave an affirming contribution to the future or damage a potential hope? Irenaeus, along with other teachers in the early church, insisted that God's plan is designed in such a way as to need human imagination and participation. The openness of the universe allows humanity the ability to "do something different." Irenaeus teaches that scripture shows that God expects humanity will learn and change, growing more and more toward God. The open view of the universe allows humanity both the luxury of doing something new as well as repenting the mistakes.

Mistakes are a part of the system, according to Irenaeus. True freedom will result in decisions that harm others either by accident or intentionally. Repentance means that at each moment God's presence in the universe requires a "candid recognition that one has made mistakes."[8] In an open universe, to keep moving into greater and greater relationship with God, there must be this candid confession.

---

7. Cox, *On Not Leaving It to the Snake*, 36.
8. Cox, *On Not Leaving It to the Snake*, 45.

The second aspect of the first step of understanding God's relationship to the universe is to affirm that there is a unity between God and creation. Irenaeus is adamant that unity does not mean that God and humanity are identical. Claims of a perfect creation, such as Augustine supported, would lead to the conclusion that creation was or at some time had been of the same substance as God because only God is perfect. Irenaeus was quite clear, the creation is creation and God is God. Using categories of the philosophy of his time, Irenaeus described the difference between humanity and God as the difference between being and becoming. Only God "is" while the rest of creation is "becoming."

Even though creation is not perfect, the relationship of God to the creation is awe inspiring, characterized by mercy and love moving from past to present and into the future. As Irenaeus writes, "For the love of God, being rich and ungrudging, confers upon the suppliant more than he can ask from it."[9] The story of creation in Genesis stands for all time as the symbolic example of the creation moment. This creation moment was the point where God, through God's will for compassion and mercy, extended the divine blessing into a created universe. This was an act of will, not of need on the part of God. God does not need to shower us with mercy. God's chooses to do so because it is the perfect expression of God's nature, which is love. As Irenaeus details:

> In the beginning, therefore, did God form Adam, not as if He stood in need of man, but that He might have [some one] upon whom to confer His benefits. For not alone antecedently to Adam, but also before all creation.[10]

Irenaeus read in the story of Genesis the response to suffering/evil and came to a very different conclusion than Augustine. God's action in creation sets the tone for God's plan, which in turn sets the stage for hope within suffering. According to Irenaeus, God in creation shows God's thought process (if you will). Through creation, God the creator and loving parent revealed God's intention that all creation, but in particular humanity, shall be exalted and come to share in the uncreated glory of God. Through this plan creation knows, "God as justice, mercy and compassion, a god who seeks us out and calls us into his own life."[11]

---

9. Irenaeus, *Against Heresies,* Book 3.Preface.
10. Irenaues, *Against Heresies,* Book IV.14:1.
11. Minns, *Irenaeus,* 34.

Becoming: God's Goal for the Creation

Some believers get carried away with the concept of an open universe. Positive thinking views tell us that humans can move forward without any serious setbacks if we just put our minds to it. This view is not acceptable to Christianity. There is a serious warning to us. "Don't get too optimistic!" There will be mistakes made within this open universe. We will be hurt as well as hurt others. As we look at the activities of humanity over the ages, the movement to God will not always be obvious nor seem to dominate human choices.

Obvious or hidden, God's plan is movement. However, human action, creativity, and imagination cannot bring God's plan to its ultimate completion. It is the Messiah, the Christ, who in returning will bring all of God's plans to perfect completion. As many have written, it remains true, "Humanity is not God." Human action will always be limited by what Irenaeus describes as the immaturity of humanity.

God's work in and unity with creation leads to the third aspect of God's relationship to creation. This third aspect is God's ongoing work to restore humanity and all creation to this unity with God. Irenaeus calls this recapitulation, or in Greek *anakaphalious*. Irenaeus grounded his understanding in passages such as Ephesians 1:9–11 where he read:

> He has made known to us the mystery of his will, according to his good pleasure that he set forth in Christ, as a plan for the fullness of time, to gather up all things in him, things in heaven and things on earth. In Christ we have also obtained an inheritance, having been destined according to the purpose of him who accomplishes all things according to his counsel and will.

Understanding the work of Christ begins with the examination of the second step of Irenaeus. Irenaeus looks for an answer to the question, "What is the nature of humanity that it experiences suffering/evil?"

STEP 2: THE NATURE OF HUMANITY

How to understand humanity is a challenge that people of faith have struggled with since Genesis 1 was first written. Today, as in past generations, there is a view of humanity that is influenced by the manner in which Augustine read these chapters. This interpretation, reviewed in Chapter Three, reads the first chapters of Genesis in a very literal manner: Adam was a real, singular individual. However, according to this view, the real person Adam sinned and that sin continues with appalling consequences for all his descendents. Through this sin, humanity lost its claim to perfection, angered God, and is now being punished.[12]

As Irenaeus and others read these chapters like Augustine and thinkers of their time, they would never have thought to question whether Adam and Eve were real individuals. What they read differently was the relationship of humanity to God. They rejected the idea that humanity is diseased or shallow. The unity that God created at the first moment of the cosmos was never lost. Irenaeus might ask, "How can you lose that which you do not have?" In contrast to the claims of a lost perfection, Irenaeus and other teachers hear Genesis telling us that the unity planned for and sought by God has yet to be fully achieved between the divine creator and the creation. It is what we might call "a work in progress."

Irenaeus reminds us that humanity, as a growing, changing creature, is as complex as God the creator. To understand our human experience of suffering/evil, an attempt must be made to reveal the components of that complexity. Irenaeus emphasizes two terms that are used in the Genesis 2:26. God creates humanity in the image (*imago*) and likeness (*similitude*) of God. As we understand what Irenaeus sees in these two terms, we find that there are two characteristics of humanity that shape human encounters of both joy and sorrow/evil. These two uniquely human characteristics are freedom and finitude. Understanding their power and limitations set up the boundaries for the answer to the question, "Why do we suffer?"

Returning again to Genesis 1:26, Irenaeus teaches us that the passage is saying something unique and of enormous significance when it says that humanity is created in the image and likeness of God. These terms connect humanity to God through the Son as well as through the Spirit. They reveal the path or unique course that God has created for humanity to move into unity with God. The teachers of the time of Irenaeus call this path divinization.

All the qualities of what it means to be human are summed up in God's words, "Let us make humankind in our image, according to our likeness." Irenaeus asked the opening question, "What does it mean to be created in the image and likeness of God?" First, it means that our human form of cells and molecules is the exact form that God used to enter into our experience. God became flesh. The very physical nature of our being

12. Note: the concept of the punishment is an interpretation of Genesis chapter 3:13–24.

is the image (*imago*) of God. In other words, humanity has the same form that God uses when God took form. Even though Christ took human form long after the creation story, Irenaeus reverses the order: God first, then humanity, because God knows all things—beginning and end at the same time.

In a similar way, Irenaeus believes that the likeness (*similitude*) of God that is described at the creation is the presence of the Holy Spirit. The Sprit of God breathes life into the earth (the mud or clay) that God has fashioned into human form. It is God's breath, the Spirit, which enables humanity to be obedient to God's will. It is the Spirit that brings the power to humanity to participate in God's plan for the cosmos. Humanity gains the likeness of God when it lives in obedience to God. The human body imitates the necessity of God's breath in how it functions. A runner or singer knows that good breathing brings power to his or her body. In response, they practice breathing techniques that will maximize their power.

Through this interpretation of Genesis, Irenaeus is confident that humanity has the possibility of growing into the perfect image and likeness of God. He is especially confident now that this perfect image and likeness has and can be seen in the life, teachings, death, and resurrection of Jesus the Christ. Irenaeus acknowledges that growth is painful.

These are exciting promises. Our very bodies are God's chosen form. Our path of growth and maturity is God's chosen path. Hope is found as we recognize that through the created nature of humanity—the image and likeness of God—humanity is in constant contact with what Irenaeus calls the two hands of God: the Son and the Spirit.

God, by choosing to create, demonstrates that humans are empowered by God to live life in God's plan. God affirms this plan by establishing a relationship with humanity through the Son. The result of God's intention is that God sees and celebrates the similarities between humanity and Christ rather than emphasizing the differences. Hope comes through seeing God's intentional work.

As a part of creating humanity in God's image and likeness, Irenaeus emphasizes that humanity is different than the rest of creation. God has planned a unique course for us women and men:

> Man receives advancement and increase towards God. For as God is always the same, so also man, when found in God, shall always go on towards God.[13]

Irenaeus shows that Genesis records the message that humanity was created by God to move toward God. God creates a process for humanity. Irenaeus and other teachers of the church call this process divinization. As the first sojourners on the path to God, the biblical Adam and Eve are not responsible for opening up the Pandora's box that released irreparable harm into the creation.

The biblical parents of humanity did not release evil into the world, as people have often heard from the teachers of the church. The actions in the garden did not infect humanity, resulting in generations of diseased creatures. Rather, Genesis describes Adam and Eve as symbols that reveal the immature or incomplete humanity that God created. They are the record of God's plan that humanity is to become ever more like God. The entire biblical myth of Eve, a serpent, and Adam is the story of children who have not yet arrived at their created identity. Leaving the garden, childbirth, learning to grown crops, fighting siblings, human wars, and all the biblical record tells us of the human life journey of gradual growth into God's plan.

Modeled on the example of God's relationship with Adam and Eve, Irenaeus writes that God's relationship with humanity contains intimate conversation, reproving, exhortation, and also freedom. In summary, being created in the image (imago) and likeness (similitude) of God means that God created humanity to grow and increase. This creation and journey of growth takes place through the work of God's two hands: the Son and the Holy Spirit. But God knew from the very start that the journey would contain joys and enormous sorrows. The two characteristics that God placed within this journey assured the presence of all possible experiences: both good and bad. Human freedom and human finitude or finiteness would influence every choice and decision that the human creature would make.

God knew, at the point of creation, that growth and increase combined with freedom could and would take many forms. Some of the forms are powerfully positive, moving toward God. Some of these forms would be equally powerful but destructive. Destructive forms fight against God's

---

13. Irenaeus, *Against Heresies*, Book IV.11.1.

Becoming: God's Goal for the Creation

compassion and love. At this point in the journey, humanity fails to attain the perfection that is God. The teachers that Irenaeus was familiar with described the source of human failure as envy and jealousy.[14]

Before thinking about failure, Irenaeus emphasized that real and true freedom is the first characteristic of humanity created in the image and likeness of God. This freedom, like everything else about humanity, is an expression of God's own nature. But what is freedom?

Irenaeus understood that freedom is more than permission from God with strings attached. It is not like your first time driving the family car (with Mom or Dad in the back seat.) Freedom:

> Is the power which enables human beings to enjoy beauty, to experience obligation and compassion, to care for friends and family, to strive for intellectual excellence, to participate in political systems, and so on.[15]

Human freedom allows for the open possibility of choosing to live by God's law or choosing to reject the promise through disbelief and disobedience.

Through the example of the apostles, Irenaeus sees the intended use of human freedom. As he writes, "(T)he apostles, who were commissioned to find out the wanderers, and to be for sight to those who saw not, and medicine to the weak."[16] The faithful believer in any generation has the opportunity, creativity, and power to use the freedom of God to do God's will. Following the writings of Paul, Irenaeus provides this longer passage:

> Therefore, also, those who are in truth His disciples, receiving grace from Him, do in His name perform [miracles], so as to promote the welfare of other men, according to the gift which each one has received from His . . . Some heal the sick by laying their hands upon them, and they are made whole . . . It is not possible to name the number of the gifts which the Church, [scattered] throughout the whole world, has received from God, . . . which she exerts day by day for the benefit of the Gentiles . . . For as she has received freely from God, freely also does she minister [to others].[17]

---

14. Clement of Rome, *First Epistle to the Corinthians*, Chapter IV. Line 18–25.
15. Farley, *Tragic Vision*, 34.
16. Irenaeus, *Against Heresies*, Book III.5.5.
17. Irenaeus, *Against Heresies*, Book II.31.4.

Irenaeus and others believe that humanity has and will continue through the ages to use freedom in ways that contribute to God's plan for unity. Each human step on the path of love and compassion brings God's kingdom into the lives of others. This is the journey toward unity with God. This is the intended human path to divinization.

Unfortunately, the possibility of disobedience shadows the life of humanity from Adam onward. The shadowed side of freedom is its internal characteristic of desire. Just as freedom allows humanity to strive to contribute to the world, it also allows us to use our creativity for no purpose other than to meet our own desires and perceived needs. Life is stressed and damaged when freedom cannot meet all the desires that we identify as necessary for our life to be beautiful and valuable.

In all lives there are many moments when our desires overcome our God-given direction for the use of freedom. The Christian church has called the resulting actions sin. Defined in many forms, for this chapter sin is the result when humanity willfully uses its freedom to satisfy selfish desires. Sin is the "unnatural occupation, through which the whole of human life is laid under the tyranny of the oppressor."[18]

When the misdirection of freedom damages an individual or community, the path to unity with God is obscured. Our connection to God is damaged or even in some cases broken. When freedom leads to sin, humanity sees itself as an individual, not one being among many. Sin encourages us to see ourselves as autonomous and separate entities rather than a creature in need of a constant connection with God and others.

Unlike Augustine's view of humanity, the reality of sin within the life of the free human does not end God's plan for humanity. Irenaeus does not see scriptures telling the story of a wrath-filled or offended God who needs to be appeased. The resulting suffering/evil is unnatural and not a part of the God-created nature of humanity.

Suffering/evil results from the action of any immature creature that has strayed from God. As we see creation today, the ongoing experience is that humanity created to increase (grow closer to God) has in reality decreased (grown closer to ultimate separation from God and eternal death).[19] While this situation brings sadness and even anger to mind, it should not reduce us to inaction.

---

18. Wingren, *Man and the Incarnation*, 43–44.
19. Wingren, *Man and the Incarnation*, 47.

Becoming: God's Goal for the Creation

This separation is not the final characteristic as Irenaeus reads the divine-human story in Genesis. Irenaeus believed that God knew that the immature, truly free human would take many wrong paths on the way to unity with God. Human frailty, that is physical as well as spiritual, is also a part of God's plan.

The second characteristic of the uniqueness of humanity created in the image and likeness of God is human finitude. All creation has a moment of beginning and a point of ending. God intended from the beginning that all creation carry this characteristic. "What is created comes into existence in time and ceases to exist in time."[20] Only God is eternal. All teachers of the church accept this point.

In the moments where humanity moves away from God, allowing envy, jealousy, uncertainty, and desire to rule life, death is a threat. When we use our freedom to serve our own needs, the concept of an end is avoided at all costs. As Irenaeus describes the immature human creature, we can call to mind a child who does not want the fun to end. Angry cries of no and "You're mean," can be heard when a child learns that he or she must leave a favorite place. Any parent can fill in a park, party, toy, or friend.

The difference in Irenaeus is that he knows that this ending is not a punishment for sin. Creatures do not need to scream and cry against the creator who made the system finite. The movement toward death is not the final path for creation. In spite of human immaturity, Irenaeus affirms that there is hope. Human creation needs to rejoice in its finitude rather than seek after God's eternity.

The final corrective in God's plan assures that in this interim time, before all is in unity with God for all time, there are moments of complete unity. Irenaeus affirms that it is the will of God that all creation will be renewed. Based upon Isaiah 11, Irenaeus wrote:

> When also the creation, having been renovated and set free, shall fructify with an abundance of all kinds of food, from the dew of heaven, and from the fertility of the earth.[21]

For Irenaeus, God is life, the divine activity is life, and all things are in the presence of life. The divine hope is that all creation experience life through and with God.

---

20. Wingren, 197.
21. Irenaeus, *Against Heresies*, Book V.33.3.

The consequences of Irenaeus's position are that God's being and creation's becoming will ultimately be identical. "These two facts are the same reality seen from two different aspects."[22] God, in perfect completion, reaches outward to creation, and immature creation grows toward God. This growth continues despite suffering/evil because God constantly surrounds humanity. As humanity sees life, it sees the creative activity of God. As humanity sees suffering and pain, it sees attempts to deny or negate the power of God.

> Whatever affects life adversely is wrong and contrary to the will of the Creator, but at the same time too it is death, something which destroys life like poison in the body.[23]

Suffering/evil finds power as its tries to interrupt and destroy the process of becoming. When evil desires dehumanizing pain, it must be resisted. Interrupting or damaging the process of human becoming is contrary to God's plan.

However, the problems in the relationship between humanity and God are not simply solved by humanity using freedom to "grow up." Even in those moments where humanity uses its freedom either as an individual or as a community to do the will of God, there is still an enormous gap between humanity and God. Suffering/evil uses this gap to dominate human existence warping freedom and pushing humanity farther from God.

STEP 3: THE WORK OF THE CHRIST

God is loving and compassionate. Humanity is created in the image and likeness of God. God's purpose for humanity and the creation is for it to be united with God. This all sounds great, but it is not the experience of us all. When life kicks us in the face, it is almost impossible to recall how we are created in God's image. When our partner is taken from us, the pain of suffering/evil prevents us from growing into God. When we are suffering, our experience tells us that suffering/evil and not God is the controlling power of creation. At these times and in their aftermath, the path back to God seems obscure and unrecognizable. It is tempting to

---

22. Wingren, *Man and the Incarnation*, 7.
23. Wingren, *Man and the Incarnation*, 14.

Becoming: God's Goal for the Creation

believe opinions that say humanity is so evil and so damaged that there is no hope.

Christian teachings reject this fatalistic view. Life is difficult and painful for many people. However, suffering/evil does not control God's creation. All Christian theology agrees that the only means to resolve the tension, bridge the gap, or repair the damage between God and humanity is through the intercession of the Christ.

While all agree that an answer to the question of suffering is found through God's entrance into the creation, the challenge continues. What is God's motivation? Are we back at the three explanations of suffering that were reviewed in Chapter Two? Are those teachers correct who say that God sent the Christ as a direct response to God's anger at humanity? Irenaeus rejects this idea. God is not angry with creation.

God continues to desire the unity with creation and the ultimate divinization of humanity. Irenaeus describes God's desire in dynamic terms of action. God acts through Jesus to bring to completion God's plan for the unity of creation. Even as God is planning to act and then acting through Christ, God sees how far off track this process has gone.

Through Christ, God took two actions. First, God re-entered history. This began the event of recapitulation. God continued the process of unity begun in the creation. Second, Irenaeus said that Christ became human so that humanity could become Christ. Divinization of humanity occurs through Christ's going over the ground of humanity.

The entry of God into the creation in the person of Jesus is called the incarnation. As God enters into human form in Jesus, history reaches its center and turning point. Irenaeus recognizes God's plan as the unfolding of a unified movement from creation, through the incarnation, crucifixion, resurrection and continuing on to the eschaton, or time of ending. Through the eons of creation, humanity's process of maturation was erratic and uncertain. At the incarnation, God offers the moment for the process to start over. The new start is called recapitulation.

In recapitulation, Irenaeus combines the ideas of a long course of human development, but not in a straight line. It is the idea of a "spiral climb."[24] God acts in Christ to gather up the entire creation and reverse its direction. This term describes the accomplishment of God's plan of salvation. As Irenaeus explains:

---

24. Lawson, *The Biblical Theology of Saint Irenaeus*, 142.

> For as through the disobedience of one man, first to be made of virgin soil, many were made sinners and lost their life; so it was necessary that by the obedience of one man, first to be born of a virgin, many should be made righteous and receive salvation. Accordingly the Word became flesh. God recapitulating the ancient creation of man in Himself, in order to slay sin, to remove death's sting, and restore man to the life.

But gathering humanity up into Christ, or completing the circle from the moment of creation back again, was not enough to bridge the gap between God and humanity. This was not enough to restore to humanity the unity that God intended. There is another part of this action of recapitulation that only Christ can accomplish. Only the Christ can become human and live the human life perfectly as God intended at the beginning.

The second action is described by Irenaeus in the opening words of book V of *Against Heresies*. "Christ became what we are so that we might become what he is." This is Irenaeus summary of God's work, plan, and very nature. When God took on human form, God transformed and irrevocably changed history.

> Thus the incarnation implies an exodus of God out of himself, while he yet stays within himself, in order to eliminate the existing gulf between God and Man. This ecstasy or movement of God is understood in terms of divine love.[25]

The work of Jesus is not to rescue humanity in some new idea that God thought of as a last-minute, desperate act. Jesus becoming human, the incarnation, is a continuation of a relationship between the Word of God and the creation.

"Thus, in and through Christ, man has the possibility of connecting himself with the perfect, divine oneness in a person and unique communion of love."[26] God began a relationship with humanity at creation. This relationship took a new step when God chose to walk among us in human form. Everything that God began in creation has pointed to this moment when God physically connected with us. The purpose of God's indwelling sums all things in the activity of Jesus's life. Ephesians 1:10 explains it all.

---

25. Scouteris, "The People of God-Its Unity and Its Glory, 410.
26. Scouteris, 404.

Becoming: God's Goal for the Creation

God "set forth in Christ, as a plan for the fullness of time, to gather up all things in Him, things in heaven and things on earth" (Eph 1:10).

The act of summing up means that Jesus lived all the experience of being human. The difference is that Jesus lived these experiences with perfect obedience to God. When Jesus encountered the pain of illness, the hostility of envy, or the determination of others to kill him, he did not misuse the freedom that he had. He chose to use God's power of love and compassion as a response to each and every experience of suffering/evil.

God's activity—coming in human form—repairs the gap between humanity and God. Through the concrete example and powerful action of Jesus, God resets the direction of humanity. In other words, first, through Jesus humanity now has a model for the use of our freedom. Jesus the Christ shows humanity the way to move forward through suffering. Second, through the resurrection of Christ, humanity learns that life does not end with the horrors of human actions.

The response to suffering is not to blame God or to blame ourselves. The model of Jesus is not one built upon shame or anger. Focusing on the power of the incarnation demonstrates the third step in the search for meaning in suffering. In the first step, God found the creation to be good and spoke words of blessing to all things. In the second step, humanity was created in the image and likeness of God imbued from creation with the desire to grow toward God. In this third step, Irenaeus tells the faithful that scripture shows that Christ is both of these: the source of blessing and the perfect image and likeness of God. As the true image and likeness of God and the "hands" through which God formed humanity and all creation, Christ is the source for the re-forming, the summing up, and the recapitulation of all things.

Humanity now has a visible plan for salvation, a visible response to suffering/evil. God's purpose is worked out perfectly in the events and experiences of the life of Jesus. Why is the suffering? Irenaeus's response is simple, "Because we are free and finite." Is this God's plan that we should suffer? Again, Irenaeus and teachers of this theological path would shout no. Asking the question of the purpose of suffering has always been the wrong question. The correct question is, "What is our response to suffering/evil?"

QUESTIONS FOR CONVERSATION AND DISCUSSION

1. Explain to another what it means to you to say that the heart of humanity is found in service of God.
2. Describe the connection between reading Genesis in a symbolic manner and accepting the premise that the creation was created in an open manner.
3. How does Irenaeus describe God's intention for creation?
4. Compare the difference between the view of humanity as fallen and Irenaeus' view of humanity as immature.
5. How does the work of the Spirit contribute to God's plan that humanity grows into the perfect image and likeness of God?
6. Some teachers claim that the difference between humanity and the rest of creation is humanity's ability to reason. Does that proposal fit into Irenaeus' perspective of humanity?
7. Is the suffering of humanity a surprise or unexpected to God?
8. What is the nature of human freedom? What is its relationship to suffering/evil?
9. In the plan of Irenaeus, suffering is defined as attempts to deny or negate the power of God. How does this relate to your understanding of a definition of sin?
10. Irenaeus gives equal emphasis to the life of Jesus and the death and resurrection. Describe the components of the model for humanity that Jesus becomes.

5

Resistance through Hope

WE HAVE ARRIVED AT an end of sorts, but also at a beginning. The maturing or divinization of humanity produces concentric or overlapping circles of action. These circles can have positive effects. When humans act in accordance with God's plan for justice and blessing for creation, the circles spread forth God's love. Positive circles of action bring humanity closer to God's plan for unity between God's self and humanity.

The circles of action can also inflict suffering that is random and unpredictable. The suffering that results falls into both categories that have been described in this book. Some people's experiences are anguish-suffering and are a part of the path of human becoming. This is the suffering of becoming. Many people experience the pain and isolation of suffering/evil that destroys humanity.

The history and study of Christianity shows that no theological method can predict suffering and allow for intervention and prevention. Faith and God's plan teach that we do not want to eliminate all anguish-suffering because these experiences assist us on the path of divinization. However, the destructive power of suffering/evil cannot be tolerated. People of faith must continue to seek answers in the face of the effects of suffering/evil in our families, communities, and world.

By this point it is clear that the traditional answers to the question of suffering/evil not only offer terrible solutions, but they actually also offer answers to the wrong question. As Robert Capon writes:

> First, they paint a picture of a very good God. Next they produce
> a grim montage of all the horrors of the world. Then, desperately,

> but gamely, they set about the thankless job of trying to reconcile the beauty of the first picture with the ugliness of the second.[1]

Previous chapters show that the answers fail because they lead to two fatal results. First, they reduce the compassionate, loving action of God into nothing more than divinely directed kind thinking. This result has the effect of saying that either God does not really care about human suffering or God feels bad that suffering happens but is not getting involved in our human drama.

The second fatal result is that these answers describe God as the unpredictable source of suffering. The argument follows that if God created everything, then God directly or indirectly created suffering/evil. Therefore God is the cause of suffering.

Neither choice is acceptable for two reasons. First, the biblical record shows God to be constant in love and compassion for the creation. God never wavers in showering blessings upon the creation. Second, it is not God's plan to leave humanity without hope for life in the present or for the future. At each generation, God reinforces God's plan through kings, prophets, Jesus, and ultimately through ordinary people who follow Christ.

The questions, "Why do we suffer?" or "What is the cause of suffering?" are both the wrong questions. The people of faith are stuck in a third-century argument because we seem to be afraid of asking the correct question. What God has been trying to get through to people for many generations is that hope is found at the time of suffering/evil when we ask of God and of ourselves, "What now?" In better form, we ask, "What are we supposed to do now that the experience of suffering/evil has reshaped our lives or the lives of those around us?"

We do not ask this question blindly. We are not crying out in the darkness with no sense of which way to go. We ask this question with the model of the life, death, and resurrection of Jesus showing us the way. When the man born blind cried out to Jesus for healing,[2] Jesus rejected the question of the disciples, "Who has sinned?" The correct question is

---

1. Capon, *The Third Peacock*, 1.

2. John 9:1–4: "As he walked along, he saw a man blind from birth. His disciples asked him, 'Rabbi, who sinned, this man or his parents, that he was born blind?' 'Neither this man nor his parents sinned. He was born blind so that God's works might be revealed in him. We must work the works of Him who sent me while it is day.'"

to ask, "What must I do for this man?" The answer modeled by the actions of the Christ is to reach out and heal those who are suffering. Jesus used his power of the compassionate love of God to restore the sight to the man born blind.

As we explore the purpose and meaning of Jesus who is the Christ, we can rewrite the three steps of the theodicy construction that we began with in Chapter One. In the first step, God reveals God's loving nature as God finds the creation to be good. God demonstrates love as God speaks words of blessing to all things. In the second step, suffering/evil exists because humanity is immature. Immature actions and choices lead to suffering. Finally, there is hope in the creation because Jesus Christ, the perfect image and likeness of God, is the source for recapitulation. Through Christ all the creation is being reformed and restored to unity with God.

Irenaeus offers us three actions that are a part of God's plan for those moments when our lives are damaged by suffering. In the first action, we search for and reaffirm the location of God. In the second action, we reject the passivity that the destructive power of suffering brings into our lives. We reject teachings that compound suffering by telling us that we can do nothing. Recapitulation gives humanity the power to move beyond the place of self-deception and casual disregard for the suffering of others.

In the third action, we fight back, but not in the manner of inflicting suffering on another. This is not a proposal that reinforces "eye for an eye" theology. We fight back using the tools of the incarnation: compassionate love and God's justice. In fighting back, we work to grow beyond the mistakes and bondage of repetition of careless action that lead to suffering. This is Resistant Hope.

LOOKING FOR GOD

At the moment that suffering/evil attempts to destroy the humanity of the sufferer, the location of God has not changed. In the face of suffering, the community confidently announces to the sufferer that God is present and at work within the creation. The victim will have difficulty believing this proclamation. It is difficult for us to look through our tears or our anger and see God. The community, as it can see more clearly, announces that as each innocent victim dies, God stands at his or her side. God is with the woman in Africa as she dies of AIDS-related pneumonia. At the same moment, God is with the family in Kansas mourning the death of their father/soldier.

Looking for God is really quite simple. We look for the signs of God's action. This is the way that the faithful have always located God. Where do we see compassionate love reaching out to those in sorrow? Where do we see people risking their own livelihood and even their own lives for others? Where do we see people giving to strangers? These are the signs of God's action. These signs are the same through all time.

The scriptural story is clear. When we seek God's presence in society, we do not need to look very far. We need to look beyond our own satisfied lives to the lives of those who are abused, downtrodden, manipulated, and persecuted by society. When we look beyond our material consumption and see those who are homeless, unemployed, or underemployed, we see the presence of God. God is and has always been most powerfully at work and most visible among people who have little or among those who place little value upon the profits of society.

In these places, we experience God's power as compassionate love. God reaches out to reaffirm the unity between God's self and the creation. The result of God's presence and continuing action is the blessing of the sufferer just as God blesses all the creation. This action continues despite the lies told to the sufferer. This blessing is God's will for humanity to reach the perfection that is total unity with God.

The blessing of God reveals the path to the sufferer. It uncovers the answer to the real question: How do we persevere in this time? The real question brought out by suffering is the question of survival. What is necessary, what is available, what is needed for the sufferer to be able to face tomorrow with a sense of personal value and hope?

As God walks through the creation with the sufferer, God encourages him or her to use the power of the incarnation to continue on the path of recapitulation. This means more than rejecting the powers of evil. God does not run a campaign of "just say *no* to evil." Recapitulation addresses the power of suffering to isolate humanity and destroy their sense of personal value through the lie that God has abandoned the victim. Recapitulation works in this place of shadows, where there is power to destroy the potential for a hope-filled life. Recapitulation overpowers this attack on humanity. Through recapitulation, the person subjected to the power of suffering/evil refuses to become a victim to its devastating messages.

Resistance through Hope

THE WORK OF RECAPITULATION: REJECTING PASSIVITY

As Irenaeus teaches us, the power of God in the creation is the living presence of Jesus the Christ. As Christ works in and through the creation, we have the example and the model that we are to follow. Following the example of Jesus, humanity uncovers two paths of resistance. The first is to name the situations that cause the suffering. The second is to resist acceptance of the inner determinism of suffering.[3] Through these two paths, hope is restored through resistance and the sufferer reconnects with God. God in turn reaffirms the incarnate power in all things and redefines meaning for creation.

The first path to recapitulation is naming. This path has two functions. First, naming raises up and reveals the places of unity with God. In the second function, naming uncovers the attempts to break, disrupt, or destroy unity between God and creation. In the action of naming, we celebrate the locations of the work of Christ as well as defy the dehumanizing attempts of suffering/evil. Naming pours light upon the true and good as well as the false and evil.

Applying Irenaeus's incarnational theology, naming reaffirms the union with God in the face of appalling pain and suffering. In answer to St. Paul's question in Romans 8:35, "Who will separate us from the love of God?" naming affirms that God is located in and surrounds the lives of sufferers. As a Christian, Irenaeus teaches that the first place that creation hears the call to compassion and justice, the naming of unity and mercy, is in the sacraments. It is in the bread and wine, body and blood, of Holy Communion and the water of Holy Baptism that God demonstrates God's action and power in the present experience of life. Resistant Hope is grounded in the knowledge that God has not abandoned the creation. As Irenaeus compares Holy Communion with human bodies:

> But our opinion is in accordance with the Eucharist . . . For as the bread, which is produced from the earth, receives the invocation of God, is no longer common bread, but the Eucharist, consisting of two realities, earthly and heavenly; so also our bodies, when they receive the Eucharist, are no longer corruptible, having the hope of the resurrection to eternity.[4]

---

3. Farley, *Tragic Vision*, 57.
4. Irenaeus, *Against Heresies*, Book 4.18.5.

The student was explaining why he was twenty-five and still in college. In his first years after high school, he encountered the Amnesty International student organization on his college campus. He found their purpose to be in sympathy with his Christian faith. Taken from the Web page for Amnesty International, its purpose is described as, "Outraged by human rights abuses but inspired by hope for a better world, we work to improve human rights through campaigning and international solidarity."[5] As he learned about the political oppression in Africa, he chose to leave college for a year to work in missions for food resources development.

Naming demands that we see hope in the face of despair. Every action that we take based in the compassionate love of Christ resists the power of suffering/evil. Hope begins to gain power when the affluent among us accept the power that we hold in society. This is the power to use resources to help others. We have the power to speak out, continuing the process of naming. In the moments when we are not the ones suffering, we are the ones with the power to speak and name the actions that would destroy others.

While naming the places of power and unity is vital, it is not enough. Christ calls our bluff when we deceive ourselves into the belief that we are compassionate for the suffering of others. In its second function, naming reveals the lies that label human life as worthless or insignificant to God. Self-deception and casual disregard are exposed in the strong, clean light of naming.

The college student on the way to Africa names our self-deception by showing us that we are ignoring the tragic suffering of others. Popular political wrangling is more often the subject of newscasts rather than the continuing genocide in Darfur. The student names our participation in the causes of suffering through our insatiable demands for control of the flow of goods, use of oil, and ignorance of the painful and frightening situations in other countries.

Closer to home, naming reveals our casual disregard for our own suffering. Naming uncovers our lies. In our affluent neighborhoods and attractive, wealthy churches, we reject the idea that we are suffering. Naming reveals the pain hidden in our neat, clean worlds. Alongside the physical and psychological abuse in our homes, naming reveals that our lives are frozen and uncreative because we have created a protective

---

5. http://www.amnesty.org/en/who-we-are.

bubble in which we live. Naming shows us that we are reduced to less than human by our intentional ignorance of the suffering in our own lives.

Each person desires a life that is calm, quiet, and safe. Naming reveals that the existence we desire is filled with self-deception that leads us into a quiet stagnation. Our longing for a life of painless satisfaction blinds us to the real needs for justice in our communities and world. Our callous choice of blindness allows suffering/evil to shape our lives. A suffocating blanket of satisfaction stifles our ability to truly perceive reality.[6]

Naming the attempts to disrupt human/divine unity is not enough to push the power of evil into retreat. Victims who are too broken and too near emotional death cannot speak with the power of the incarnate Christ. Then the second path of resistance must be followed by those who are well, those who are not dying at this moment under the onslaught of evil work.

These are faithful yet wounded brothers and sisters who shoulder the responsibility to resist the inner working of suffering. Through personal and public means, they resist through a two-step process. The first step, recollection, is the personal and public retelling of memory. These are the stories that raise up hope by honoring words and actions. The second step is reenactment. The faithful, filled with the power of the stories, reenact those memories in their own contemporary context. In other words, we take the memories and make them powerfully our own here and now.

Christ shows us that we must push back against all attempts to define the inner meaning of humanity by emphasizing the disconnection between God and creation. Suffering/evil emphasizes the isolation of the victim. "You are alone in your pain," is the quiet and insistent message. Recollection and reenactment fight back against these insidious messages that are working to destroy humanity.

The message promoted by suffering/evil works to dehumanize by destroying dignity. We participate in this process each day through the language we choose to describe a person, such as calling a person an illegal alien rather than by his or her name. We minimize the horror of suffering by refusing to use words that name their pain. Words like rape, genocide, or holocaust are purged from public vocabulary. Our actions leave the victim without any shred of human identity.

---

6. Soelle, *Suffering*, 39.

Resistant Hope grounds recollection of stories in the dangerous memory of God's actions through the incarnation.[7] The collective memory celebrates in tradition and history the hope of the personal relationship of God through the incarnation. Christmas is not a season; it is an event that changes history forever. Easter is not a special Sunday; it is the promised end to the human journey. Christ is in the world and Christ has turned all creation to a new path. As we recall or recollect the power of God's presence in human form, Christ reveals the path of resistance to evil.

We know the power of recollection. In every community and every family, we tell the stories. Even the news media contributes at least in the holiday seasons. The mother tells the story of grandmother's first ride at the front of the bus. She recites the message that Grandmother was human, important, and valuable to society. The father tells the story of his time in military service for his country. He describes sharing candy with children to help demonstrate his respect for the culture of another people. The child tells the story of comforting another child who was crying in school. Even at a young age, he values the life of another child.

These are the simple stories. There are the more complicated ones told through Holocaust museums, war memorials, food banks, shelters, and free medical clinics. There are horrifying stories of dead bodies buried in secret graves, child soldiers, and women forced into prostitution. These stories must be told. When we tell them, through recollection we remember that each story is in part our story. We have either contributed to the problem or are working for a solution.

The power of suffering/evil to destroy the humanity of others is diminished when through recollection the power of Christ refreshes and restores the union between God and creation. Recollection becomes reconnection. As this reconnection flourishes, God directs human attention away from questions of "Why?" These questions only paralyze humanity and keep us captive in the darkness of suffering. Through recollection humanity experiences, "Resuscitation of the capacity to recognize another person as human, possibly even in the midst of a tragically structured environment."[8]

Telling stories is the first step in resisting the power of suffering/evil. The reunion of God and humanity turns our attention toward God's call

---

7. Farley, *Tragic Vision*, 127.
8. Farley, *Tragic Vision*, 38.

for action. In the second step of reenactment, Jesus the Christ empowers us to enact God's message of love and compassion within the creation. Reenactment becomes an open defiance. Humanity, through the power of the incarnation, carries God's love into the world. Humanity challenges claims by suffering/evil that it controls all society. Hope is found in the claim that life in the present can be lived as Christ lives, with love and compassion. As one sees the suffering of others, there is the call to redouble one's efforts and fight back.

Reenactment can be very simple. At the door of faculty offices at a small college, the observant visitor sees small, colored triangles stuck on the doorframe. In quiet action, the troubled student knows that these triangles indicate that this faculty person is safe to talk with about matters of sexuality and personal identity. The windows of the connecting hallway have become a public forum for protest. Each month they inform and challenge all who pass by to learn about breast cancer, forced prostitution, economic hardships for farmers, and other social issues.

Reenactment becomes prophetic when it moves the faithful forward to accept the cycle of life—death—new life. When reenactment becomes truly prophetic, it is the territory of dangerous witness. There are many stories of ordinary people whose lives and deaths come to our attention because they have lived out a prophetic reenactment of God's plan.

Ofelia Ortega writes of the death of Bishop Juan José Gerardi in Guatemala in 1998. Bishop Gerardi championed the rights of victims. As Ortega records:

> Just two days before he was killed, he had stood in the front of the same cathedral and prophetically warned that the church's mission was a dangerous undertaking. He said, "We want to contribute to the construction of a country that must be different. That is why we are recovering the memory of people . . . This path has been and continues to be full of risks, but the construction of the Reign of God is a risky task."[9]

We will not all be martyred for our reenactment of God's love. We cannot all go somewhere foreign and serve. Some of us will stay home. We reenact through our financial support of others. We reenact when, coming full circle, we tell the stories of the world of others.

---

9. Ortega, *Hope for the World*, 130.

Irenaeus affirms Resistant Hope is present in nature and history. It is concretized in the activities and rituals of the faith where people celebrate and proclaim that the incarnate Word, Jesus the Christ, recapitulates all things. Even when ambiguous or confusing, tradition and scripture mediated through the church and communities preserve and make holy the memories of victims of suffering. In these memories, new generations learn and experience the power of the incarnation. In the act of recollection, new generations learn to reenact God's incarnate power confronting evil and suffering of their time and place.

Where we act out God's love is both personal and communal. This book cannot tell you where you should place your energy. Jesus calls us to work in the vineyard. College students sell candy for Amnesty International. They are working to resist suffering through hope. Children collecting recyclable cans are working to resist suffering by restoring the community. The point is that we must each get our hands dirty. As we actively reenact God's compassionate love in the world, we fill the places where suffering/evil brings the darkness of hopelessness. Each community with clean water, food, a home, a family, each person with dignity and valued humanity, and each child of God valued, loved, and protected by others is less likely to use a weapon to take those things.

WHERE DOES IT END?

The teaching of Irenaeus describes humanity as moving ever closer to God. Christ has restored us to the path of divinization. However, looking at our society brings little comfort. Each day we hear more stories about suffering/evil and its power to dehumanize. It is again an example of the power of evil that we might believe that our efforts do no good. As people of faith, we must fight back against the apathy the suffering/evil would promote.

To ask about an end in our lifetime is to discourage us from working. We are tempted to wait for God to interrupt and solve the problem of human suffering. Orfelia Oretega writes that we have a different question to be answered here and now. What is our objective now, in the present? Our objective is "to develop in our students the kind of consciousness that will enable them to exercise a critical and prophetic function within the church as well as in society."[10] Our task now is to teach and demonstrate to others the power of Resistant Hope to restore dignity and value to sufferers.

As people of faith, the present time is again only temporary. It is not the conclusion to God's plan. In faith and hope, scripture teaches that at the eschaton, the end of time, there will be an end to evil and suffering. When God's plan comes to completion, all creation will be in perfect unity with God. Until that time, humanity must live with and through the power of Jesus present in the world to name suffering and act out against its attempts to dehumanize others and us. Resistant Hope that looks for God, names unity, and reenacts love is the sign in history that God's redemptive power is incarnate in all things.

---

10. Bruggemann, in *Hope for the World*, 131.

QUESTIONS FOR CONSIDERATION AND DISCUSSION

1. How do you feel about a god whose response to suffering is "kind thinking" or lack of involvement?
2. Does suffering come from God?
3. How do you actualize the step of looking for God?
4. How do you reject passivity by recollecting stories?
5. What is your favorite story that demonstrates a person fighting against suffering?
6. How do you fight back against suffering/evil's attempts to dehumanize yourself or others?

6

The Beginning

THERE ARE FOUR PARTS to the construction of Resistant Hope. The first part begins with the affirmation that the work of humanity is to participate with God in the perfecting of creation. God's plan includes our active participation. This is the way of God's creation from the very beginning as recorded in Genesis 1. Humanity, created in the image and likeness of God, is blessed. This blessing of compassionate love establishes the path along which immature humanity is to grow into unity with God. Even though humanity will stray from the path of unity through the work of the two hands of God (the Son and the Spirit), renewal will flourish.

Resistant Hope reveals the abnormality that sets in when we cease to view our actions as having any good effect upon the world. It shows how suffering/evil gains power when we diminish the critical importance of human action within God's eternal plan. Resistant Hope celebrates the continuum of God's action from creation to incarnation, through life and death, to resurrection. It rejects claims that God desires for the creation to suffer in silent abasement waiting for the end to come.

In the second part, Resistant Hope recalls through powerful acclamation that it is God's intention for the creation to join with God. God creates humanity for this specific purpose: the maturing of humanity into God. As humanity matures as individuals and communities, the hope of God's compassionate love grows stronger. God uses and works through the maturing humanity to bring justice to the oppressed, sight to the blind, and healing to those who suffer. These actions of God's justice are not restricted to the work of Christ alone. Through God's plan, they are the work of Resistant Hope as it rejects the power of suffering/evil.

In the third part, Resistant Hope reminds us that humanity lives with limitations. Humanity cannot follow the path of Resistant Hope through strength of personal will or stubborn determination. Resistant Hope does not try to cover or gloss over human mistakes that contribute to suffering/evil. It reminds us that humanity is immature. This immaturity leaves humanity open to the influences of anxiety, greed, envy, and lust for control over our own lives as well as the lives of others.

Irenaeus of Lyon teaches that human perfecting requires God's action in recapitulation. Claiming the power of recapitulation is the fourth part of the work of Resistant Hope. Jesus the Christ is incarnate in creation. Christ's living presence brings the creative power of God to sum up or recapitulate all experiences. Human life has a model to follow and a new start on the path to mature into God.

Resistant Hope is not a destination. It is not a place where people of faith need to arrive to be perfect or complete. It is a path through life or a way to view the world. When Resistant Hope grounds our point of view, we find new meaning in familiar passages of scripture. The human attitude of passivity, which is often grounded in scripture, is challenged. In addition, we are given a new understanding of God's call to endure in the face of suffering.

Christians have been encouraged for generations that they are to be passive before God. Passages such as Romans 12:12 are used to reinforce this attitude. This verse is often translated, "Rejoicing in hope, patient in suffering, and persistent in prayer." As it is then preached and taught, Christians hear Paul giving an admonition to passive waiting. People of faith are not to act in a hasty manner. Resistant Hope teaches us that rather than passivity, these words call us, the faithful, to show endurance in suffering.

Many other passages are used to encourage the attitude of passive acceptance. Those eager for action are often cautioned to "wait upon the Lord." This idea is taken from many places but one of the most common is Psalm 27:14:

> Wait for the LORD;
> be strong and let your heart take courage;
> wait for the LORD (Ps 27:14)!

Resistant Hope challenges us to examine the context in Psalm 27. The author is calling upon God to teach the prayerful supplicants and to lead them on the right paths. This is not a prayer for passivity. It is prayer that affirms God's offers of training for action. Immature human interpretation warns us that we should not act before we are confident of where

God is leading us. Resistant Hope reveals that calls for caution are often expanded into the passivity of self-absorption and disregard of the suffering of others.

Along with challenges to passivity, Resistant Hope redefines the meaning of endurance. The endurance called for by Paul and expected by God is the endurance of the Olympic athlete. We are to train and practice so that we can push back against suffering/evil as it attempts to limit us in any way. Resistant Hope stretches the limits placed upon us by suffering/evil by responding with God's previously untapped power.

Through the four parts of Resistant Hope and the new understanding of God's call to endurance and patience, humanity is set on a new path. Resistant Hope reminds us that for humanity to stay on this path, we must accept three demands that God makes upon humanity. First, God demands that humanity see God's imprint in all people. Second, God demands that we name all attempts to oppress others. In particular, God calls us to uncover those attempts where we participate in dehumanizing actions. Finally, God demands that we resist the evil that tries to destroy God's creation. God does not tolerate passivity and inaction.

FINAL THOUGHTS

Accepting that suffering is God's way to shape us into better humans is an insult to God. Accepting the world's belief that we are just getting what we deserve is an insult to who we are as God's beloved children. Resisting these destructive powers is God's goal for humanity. Resisting and pushing back the powers that would destroy us is the model that God gives to us in the life and work of Christ. Here is our redemption. Here is our hope. God has not left us powerless in this life to be pushed and damaged or ridden with guilt waiting for the release of death. God gives us God's compassionate love so that we can participate in God's plan to bring mercy and justice to the creation.

As you reach the end of this project, you have read material that might be new to you. It is not, however, new to the Christian community. The Christian church has throughout history made choices about which ideas are endorsed and which will be discarded. Too often those choices reflect the power and influence of the church, not the truth that they contain. I believe that God's purpose for each of us is that we live in justice and use God's power of compassionate love to fight on behalf of those who are oppressed. I hope that as you conclude this small project, you will be inspired to learn more about the call of God to fight against the powers of suffering and evil. Ultimately I hope that you will find a new freedom in your own life to resist and push back against personal suffering that would reduce you to less that what God intends: loved and free.

Glossary of Terms

Amnesty International: A worldwide organization whose primary purpose is to campaign for internationally recognized human rights for all.

Anguish-suffering: Suffering that results from the common experiences of life such as death, illness, or accident.

Apostles: The title given in the gospels to the twelve chief disciples of Jesus.

Augustine of Hippo (354–450): Bishop in the early church who was and continues to be an influential teacher. Augustine's teachings on original sin, the Holy Trinity and the fall of humanity continue to shape Christian teachings.

BCE/CE: Before Common Era/Common Era designate the numbering and period of time. The Common Era began with year 1 of the Gregorian calendar. These terms replaced BC (Before Christ) and AD (year of our Lord).

Buddhism and Buddha: One of the world religions based upon the teachings of Siddhartha Gautama, known as Buddha.

C.S. Lewis: Noted scholar and teacher of Medieval and Renaissance Literature at Oxford and Cambridge who converted to Christianity at the age of thirty. His works are known for their focus on Christian teachings.

Cannabis: The plant from which marijuana is extracted.

Glossary of Terms

Christ: The Greek word used to translate the Hebrew word that means messiah. It is a title that the Christian community uses as a proper name for Jesus, the Messiah, Son of God.

Christian: Name that was first applied to the followers of Jesus the Christ by those outside of the community.

Crucifixion: Roman form of capital punishment. It is believed that death resulted from asphyxiation when the accused was nailed or bound to a cross. The cross was either T-shaped or X-shaped.

Darfur: Region of far western Sudan. It borders Central African Republic, Libya, and Chad. In the twenty-first century, it is the midst of genocide and humanitarian emergency.

Doctrine: The word means teaching. Specifically it refers to the body of information that describes the accepted body of beliefs held universally by the Christian church.

Dominion: Supreme authority. In Genesis 1:26, humanity is given dominion over creation.

Dorothee Soelle (1929–2003): German theologian with focus on the engagement of faith with social and political concerns.

Douglas John Hall: Professor of Christian Theology, Faculty of Religious Studies, McGill University, Montreal, Canada.

Eastern Orthodoxy: The second largest single Christian communion in the world. It is considered by scholars to be the least changed from its ancient theological roots, which stretch back to the beginnings of Christianity. Members do not usually refer to themselves as "Eastern" Orthodox but rather with a prefix of their nation of origin such as Greek Orthodox, Russian Orthodox, or other.

Emmanuel Levinas (1906–1995): Philosopher with emphasis on Continental philosophy and studies of the Hebrew Talmud.

Eschaton: The point or time when all things come to an end or the final destiny of the world.

Glossary of Terms

Evil: Broad term used to describe actions that are cruel, unjust, or selfish.

Genesis: The opening book of the Old Testament. It contains the stories of creation and the early pre-history of humankind.

Gospel: Word meaning good news. Christianity identifies the first four books of the New Testament as gospels because each contains the central revelation of Christianity that Jesus Christ is the Son of God and the source of redemption for creation.

Holocaust: A sacrifice with many victims.

Hope: The search, desire, or in some contexts confidence for good in the future.

Incarnation: The Christian teaching that the eternal God took on human flesh in one historical instance. Jesus, God in human form, was fully and truly human.

Irenaeus of Lyon (130–200): Teacher and bishop for the early church. He was born in Smyrna and commissioned to serve in Lyon.

Israel: The most common name in the Old Testament for the land where the chosen people live. It is also the name for the Northern Kingdom that was destroyed by the invading armies of Assyria in 722.

Jeremiah (seventh century BCE): Prophet of Judah, the Southern Kingdom.

Judah: The name for the Southern kingdom that was destroyed in 587 BCE by the armies of Nebuchadnezzar of Babylon.

Metaphor: Using a word or an idea to show a comparison that in turn draws a parallel between the concepts (e.g., the Internet is an information superhighway).

Myanmar: The largest country by geographical area in mainland Southeast Asia. Formerly named Burma.

Glossary of Terms

Myth: There are many definitions. Reflecting the usage in this project, myth is a sacred story that draws together belief and contains rules for moral behavior.

Omnipotent: All-powerful or possession of the perfect form of power. Attributed only to God.

Original sin: Universal and hereditary sinfulness of all humanity since Adam and Eve.

Pain: An unpleasant physical, sensory, or emotional experience associated with possible or actual damage to self.

Paul: Apostle to the Gentiles. A Jew who converted to Christianity after Jesus revealed himself to Paul. Paul went on to found churches in Asia Minor. Paul authored seven books in the New Testament.

Pastor: Literally one who keeps animals. Used in a figurative manner to identify those called by God to care for and lead God's people.

Psalms: Songs also referring to a collection poetic songs in the Old Testament.

Rabbi: Title applied to teachers and others of revered positions. Rabbi is common title used to address the leader of a synagogue or Jewish community.

Rape: When an individual is forced to engage in activities against his or her will through threats or fear tactics. This term usually refers to forms of sexual assault.

Recapitulation: Literal meaning of summing up. Jesus recapitulated or summed up perfectly all that God intended humanity to be and become.

Resurrection: Fundamental teaching of Christianity that Jesus Christ was raised by God from the dead and is now exalted with God.

Romans: This is the longest of the letters written by Paul to help shape new Christian communities. Formal title is Epistle to the Romans.

Glossary of Terms

Scripture: The written books of sacred text. In Christianity, scripture is often used as a synonym for the Bible.

Sudan: The largest country in Africa

The Diary of Anne Frank: Record of the experiences of a young girl in the Netherlands as she and her family hid from the occupying Nazi army.

Theodicy: The attempt to justify the goodness of God in the face of the evil present in the world.

Theology: Literally it means discourse about God. In practical application, it encompasses the study of the contents of belief using reason that is enlightened by faith.

Virginia Tech: On April 16, 2007, at Virginia Polytechnic Institute and State University, a student conducted a mass shooting, killing thirty-two people.

Vocation: The call in Christianity to serve one's neighbor. Christianity teaches that God gifts each individual with unique resources and abilities that are to be used on behalf of others.

Wendy Farley: Professor of Religion at Emory University, Atlanta, Georgia.

Bibliography and Recommended Reading List

THOSE MATERIALS THAT WERE used in this book are marked with an asterisk. All others can contribute to understanding the many paths of Christian and biblical theology.

Achtemeier, Paul. *HarperCollins Bible Dictionary.* New York: HarperCollins, 1996.

Attridge, Harold, W. *HarperCollins Study Bible, Revised.* Society of Biblical Literature, New York: HarperCollins, 2006.

*Augustine. *The Works of Saint Augustine, Sermons.* Translated, Edmund Hill, O.P. Editor John E. Rotelle O.S.A., New York: New York Press, 1990.

*Beker, J. Christiaan. *Suffering and Hope: The Biblical Vision of the Human Predicament.* Philadelphia: Fortress Press: 1987.

*Bellis, Alice Ogden. *Helpmates, Harlots and Heroes: Women's Stories in the Hebrew Bible.* Louisville: Westminster/John Knox Press, 2007.

Bright, John. *History of Israel Fourth Edition.* Louisville: Westminster/John Knox, 2001.

*Brueggemann, Walter. *Genesis: Interpretation: A Bible Commentary for Teaching and Preaching.* Atlanta: John Knox Press, 1982.

*Brueggemann, Walter. Editor, *Hope for the World.* Louisville:Westminster/John Knox, 2001.

Bibliography and Recommended Reading List

*Capon, Robert Farrar. *The Third Peacock*. San Francisco: Harper and Row, 1986.

*Clement of Rome, *First Epistle to the Corinthians*, Christian Classics Ethereal Library.

*Cox, Harvey. *On Not Leaving It To The Snake*. New York: The MacMillan Company, 1967.

*Davis, Stephen. Editor, *Encountering Evil: Live Options in Theology*. Louisville: Westminster/John Knox, 2001.

*Farley, Wendy. *Tragic Vision and Divine Compassion*. Louisville: Westminster/John Knox, 1990.

*Grant, Robert M. *Irenaeus of Lyons*. New York: Routledge, 2000.

*Hall, Douglas John. *God and Human Suffering*. Minneapolis: Augsburg, 1986.

*Hick, John. *Evil and the God of Love*. London: Macmillan 1966.

*Irenaeus of Lyon. *Against Heresies*. Translated, Philip Schaff. Grand Rapids: Christian Classics Ethereal Library.

*Kushner, Harold S. *When Bad Things Happen to Good People*. New York: Quill, 2001.

*Lawson, John. *The Biblical Theology of Saint Irenaeus*. Eugene Oregon: Wipf and Stock Publishers, 2006.

*Levinas, Emmanuel. *On Thinking-of-the-Other* entre nous. New York: Columbia: University Press, 1998.

*Lewis, C. S. *The Problem of Pain*. San Francisco: Harper, 2001.

———. *A Grief Observed*. San Francisco: Harper, 2001.

Bibliography and Recommended Reading List

*Minns, Denis. *Irenaeus*. Washington, D.C.: Georgetown University Press, 1994.

*Papageorgiou, Fr. Panayiotis. "Chrysostom and Augustine on the Sin of Adam and Its Consequences," *St Vladimir's Theological Quarterly*, number 34.04, 361–78.

Platinga, Alvin. God, Freedom, and Evil. Grand Rapids, Michigan: Wm. B. Eerdmans, 1977.

*Scouteris, Constantine. "The People of God—Its Unity and Its Glory: A discussion of John 17:17–24 in the Light of Patristic Thought," *Greek Orthodox Theological Review* 30, Winter, 1985.

Sittser, Gerald L. A Grace Disguised. Grand Rapids, Michigan: Zondervan Publishing House, 1996.

*Sölle, Dorothee. *Suffering*. Philadelphia: Fortress Press, 1973.

*Tarq, Russel, Hurtak, J. J. *The End of Suffering: Fearless Living in Troubled Times*. Charlottesville, VA: Hampton Roads Publishing Company, Inc., 2006.

*Wingren, Gustaf. *Man and the Incarnation*. Philadelphia: Muhlenberg Press, 1959.

www.ingramcontent.com/pod-product-compliance
Lightning Source LLC
Chambersburg PA
CBHW070516090426
42735CB00012B/2810